Mifflin Harcourt

Test Preparation

Grade 2

Printed in the U.S.A.

ISBN 978-0-544-26854-8

1 2 3 4 5 6 7 8 9 10   0982   22 21 20 19 18 17 16 15 14 13

4500438424   A B C D E F G

Dear Parent or Educator,

Welcome to *Core Skills: Test Preparation*. You have selected a book that will help your child develop the skills he or she needs to succeed on standardized tests.

Although testing can be a source of anxiety for children, this book will give your child the preparation and practice that he or she needs to feel better prepared and more confident when taking a standardized test. Research shows that children who are acquainted with the scoring format of standardized tests score higher on those tests. Students also score higher when they practice and understand the skills and strategies needed to take standardized tests. The subject areas and concepts presented in this book are typically found on standardized tests at this grade level.

To best help your child, please consider the following suggestions:

- Provide a quiet place to work.
- Go over the directions and the sample exercises together.
- Review the strategy tips.
- Reassure your child that the practice tests are not "real" tests.
- Encourage your child to do his or her best.
- Check the lesson when it is complete.
- Go over the answers and note improvements as well as problems.

If your child expresses anxiety about taking a test or completing these lessons, help him or her understand what causes the stress. Then, talk about ways to eliminate anxiety. Above all, enjoy this time you spend with your child. He or she will feel your support, and test scores will improve as success in test taking is experienced.

Help your child maintain a positive attitude about taking a standardized test. Let your child know that each test provides an opportunity to shine.

Sincerely,

The Educators and Staff of
Houghton Mifflin Harcourt

P.S. You might want to visit our website at **www.hmhco.com** for more test preparation materials as well as additional review of content areas.

Core Skills: Test Preparation

GRADE 2

Contents

Standardized Test Content Areas

Reading Skills

*Identifying compound words

*Identifying correct word endings

*Identifying contractions

*Recognizing and matching consonant sounds, consonant blends, consonant digraphs, short and long vowel sounds, vowel diphthongs, vowel digraphs, and r-controlled vowels

Identifying synonyms

*Using sentence context to determine meaning of multiple-meaning words

*Using sentence context to determine word meaning

*Interpreting the main idea

*Recalling specific details

Making inferences

Drawing conclusions

*Extending meaning

*Identifying actions, reasons, and sequence

Understanding cause and effect

Predicting outcomes

*Using definitional phrases to determine word meanings

*Relating pictures to stories

+Identifying sequence

Language Skills

*Remembering stated details, sequences, and directions

Drawing conclusions

Making inferences

*Recognizing literary elements such as rhyme in poems

Distinguishing between reality and fantasy

*Distinguishing between clearly written sentences and those that contain errors in expression and construction

*Determining topic relevance and organizing information

Alphabetizing words

*Using a table of contents to locate information in a book

*Determining correct sentence order

*Identifying extraneous information within a paragraph

*Identifying correctly applied grammar

*Identifying correct capitalization and punctuation

*Identifying correctly and effectively written sentences

*Identifying misspelled words in sentences

Mathematics Skills

*Identifying numbers

Identifying ordinal position

*Comparing and ordering numbers

Understanding expanded notation and place value

*Recognizing odd and even numbers

*Understanding properties of whole numbers and the fundamental operations

+Identifying parts of a whole and of a set

+Recognizing number and shape patterns

*Counting

*Reading and interpreting pictographs, tables, and tally charts

Determining simple probability

*Identifying geometric shapes

*Understanding basic properties of plane, congruent, and symmetrical figures

Identifying rotations and reflections

*Using standard and nonstandard units to estimate and to measure

*Identifying appropriate measurement units

*Telling time to the nearest quarter hour

Reading a calendar

*Determining the value of groups of coins

*Applying units of money

*Identifying operations

*Using problem-solving strategies to solve word problems

*Applying addition and subtraction to word problems

*Adding and subtracting whole numbers

*Aligns to Grade 2 Common Core State Standards.

+Extension: Aligns to Grade 3 Common Core State Standards.

iv

Core Skills: Test Preparation

INTRODUCTION

Standardized tests are becoming increasingly more important in both public and private schools, yet test anxiety causes many children to perform below their fullest potential. *Core Skills: Test Preparation* is designed to help children succeed on standardized tests. This program refreshes basic skills, familiarizes children with test formats and directions, and teaches test-taking strategies.

A large part of being well prepared for a test is knowing how to approach different types of questions and learning how to use time wisely. *Core Skills: Test Preparation* gives children the opportunity to take a test under conditions that parallel those they will face when taking standardized tests. This practice and experience will allow them to feel more confident when taking standardized tests and will enable them to demonstrate their knowledge successfully.

Tools for Success

Core Skills: Test Preparation gives children valuable practice with the content areas and question formats of the major standardized tests used nationally.

Core Skills: Test Preparation provides the following:
- Test-taking strategies
- Familiarity with test directions
- Review of skills and content
- Awareness of test formats
- Practice tests

Organization

The book is divided into units that correspond to those found on standardized tests.
- Reading Comprehension
- Reading Vocabulary
- Mathematics Problem Solving
- Listening
- Language

Core Skills: Test Preparation is designed to ensure success on test day by offering the following:

Test-Taking Strategies

Unit 1 provides valuable test-taking strategies to help your child do his or her best on the reading portion of any standardized test.

Targeted Reading Objectives

Unit 2 focuses on six reading objectives. Each page contains a definition, tip, or hint to help your child master the targeted objective.

Mathematics Problem Solving

Unit 5 offers a step-by-step approach to solving math word problems.

Skill Lessons

The skill lessons contained in Units 3, 4, 6, 7, and 8 prepare your child by providing both content review and test-taking strategies. Each skill lesson includes the following:

Directions—clear, concise, and similar to those found on standardized tests;

Try This—a skill strategy that enables children to approach each lesson exercise in a logical way;

A **Sample**—to familiarize children with test-taking items;

Think It Through—a specific explanation of the correct answer in the sample item; and

A **Practice Section**—a set of exercises based on the lesson and modeled on the kinds of exercises found on standardized tests.

Unit Tests

These tests cover all the skills from the lessons.

Practice Tests

The last five units in the book, Units 9–13, are the **Practice Tests**. These tests simulate the situations that your child will encounter when taking standardized tests.

Using This Book

Try This and Think It Through Features

The **Try This** and **Think It Through** features accompany the sample questions on the skill lesson pages. Before your child answers the sample question, go over the **Try This** skill strategy by reading it aloud. Give your child time to answer the question, and then review the correct answer using the **Think It Through** feature.

Scripts

Most of the lessons, unit tests, and practice tests in this book contain scripted material that must be read aloud by an adult to the child. Adult involvement is required because many children at this age are still developing their reading skills, and scripted material prevents reading difficulties from interfering with the testing of content areas. Those sections that practice or test the child's reading ability are, of course, not scripted.

All the necessary scripts, as well as all the answers, have been collected in the section called **Scripts and Answers**, pages 129–162. This section has been perforated so that you can remove it easily. Your child can mark his or her answers in the book while you read from the scripted pages.

Practice Tests

The five practice tests, pages 96–127, simulate standardized tests, providing your child with valuable practice before test day. Like many standardized tests, these are timed. The following are the suggested times needed to administer each test:

Reading Comprehension	35 minutes
Reading Vocabulary	20 minutes
Math Problem Solving	50 minutes
Listening	25 minutes
Language	35 minutes

Answer Bubbles

You may want to go over how to fill in the multiple choice bubble-in answers. Stress the importance of filling the answer bubble completely, pressing firmly, and erasing any stray marks.

Short Answer Questions

Standardized tests also require children to answer questions using their own words. *Core Skills: Test Preparation* gives children practice answering this type of question.

Individual Record Form

The **Individual Record Form** found on page 128 can be used to track progress through the book and to record the child's scores on the lessons, unit tests, and practice tests.

Icons

This book contains the following icons to help you and your child:

 The **Go On** icon tells your child to continue on to the next page.

 The **Stop** icon tells your child to stop working.

 The stopwatch icon indicates the amount of time to allot for each **Practice Test**.

Core Skills: Test Preparation lessons and practice provide children with the tools they need to build their self-confidence. That self-confidence can translate into a positive test-taking experience and higher scores on standardized tests. With its emphasis on skills, strategies for success, and practice, *Core Skills: Test Preparation* gives children the ability to succeed on standardized tests.

Unit 1
Reading Test-Taking Strategies

These strategies will help you do your best on reading tests. They will help you organize the information needed to answer the questions.

STRATEGY 1
The Check and See Strategy

This strategy can be used when a question asks for a fact from the passage. The answer to the question is in the passage. It is not hidden. Some of the same words may be in the passage and in the question.

 Check and See will help you answer *remembering information* questions.

This is the Check and See Strategy

1. **READ: Read** the question.

2. **FIND: Find** the words you need in the passage.

3. **DECIDE: Decide** which strategy to use.
   Check and See: Put a **check** next to the sentence where you can **see** the words you need to answer the question.

4. **ANSWER:** Choose the best **answer.**

STRATEGY 2
The Puzzle Piece Strategy

This strategy can be used when a question asks you what something means. Sometimes there does not seem to be an answer. It is not stated in the passage.

 Puzzle Piece helps you put facts together to get the answer. This is like putting a puzzle together. Puzzles are made up of many pieces. You cannot look at one piece and know what the picture is. Only when you put the pieces together can you see the whole picture.

This is the Puzzle Piece Strategy

1. **READ: Read** the question.

2. **FIND: Find** the facts you need in the passage.

3. **DECIDE: Decide** which strategy to use.
   Write: Write the facts in puzzle pieces.
   Put Together: Put the puzzle pieces **together** to see the picture.

4. **ANSWER:** Choose the best **answer.**

STRATEGY 3
The What Lights Up Strategy

This is another strategy you can use when an answer is not in the passage. You need to add your own ideas to the passage.

 What Lights Up can help you see if something is real, useful, or a fact. It can show you what would happen if the story had a different ending.

You can use the **What Lights Up Strategy** to answer the hardest type of question. This is when you are asked to read and think of your own ideas.

This is the What Lights Up Strategy

1. **READ: Read** the question.

2. **FIND: Find** the facts you need in the passage.

3. **DECIDE: Decide** which strategy to use.
   Write: Write the facts in the book.
   Think: Think about your own ideas.
   Light Up: Think about what you have
          written. The answer will
          light up in your mind.

4. **ANSWER:** Choose the best **answer.**

5

STOP

Unit 2: Reading Comprehension

SPECIFIC OBJECTIVES

Objective 1: **Determining word meanings**
Suffixes, context clues, and technical words

Objective 2: **Identifying supporting ideas**
Recalling facts and details, sequential order,
following directions, and describing settings

Objective 3: **Summarizing main ideas**
Stated main ideas and identifying summaries

Objective 4: **Perceiving relationships and recognizing outcomes**
Cause-and-effect and making predictions

Objective 5: **Making inferences and generalizations**
Inferring information and drawing conclusions

Objective 6: **Recognizing points of view, facts, and opinions**
Discerning facts and points of view

OBJECTIVE 1: DETERMINING WORD MEANINGS

Suffixes are parts of some words. A *suffix* is at the end of a word. You can use suffixes to tell what the words mean.

Our class went on a trip to the zoo. We saw some monkeys climb into a tree. One monkey climbed <u>higher</u> than the others.

1. In this paragraph, the word <u>higher</u> means —

○ more than high.

○ lower.

○ almost as high.

○ on the ground.

Hint: The suffix "er" means more than.

Goldilocks walked into the three bears' home. She sat down at their table. She would not eat Papa Bear's food because it was the <u>warmest</u>.

2. In this paragraph, the word <u>warmest</u> means —

○ the least warm.

○ more than warm.

○ the most warm.

○ cool.

Hint: The suffix "est" means the most.

José walked up to the starting line for the foot race. He really wanted to win. José knew how important it was to run <u>quickly</u>. At the sound of the "bang" the race began.

3. In this paragraph, the word <u>quickly</u> describes —

○ how he will walk.

○ how he wanted to win.

○ how the race began.

○ how he will run.

Hint: When you see "ly" at the end of a word, it usually describes an action word.

STOP

7

Mei was getting ready for her birthday party. She invited all of her friends to come. Mei and her mother baked the cupcakes. They were very excited about her party.

4. In this paragraph, the word baked means —

○ the cupcakes were made already.

○ the cupcakes were not made yet.

○ they were making the cupcakes now.

○ they will not bake the cupcakes.

Hint: The suffix "ed" shows that something has already happened.

Angela's class went to the school library to take its class picture. Angela was tall, so she stood in the second row. Her friend Sulky was taller, so she stood in the third row.

5. In this paragraph, the word taller means —

○ more than tall.

○ the most tall.

○ not tall at all.

○ the least tall.

Hint: When you see "er" at the end of a word, what does that mean?

Kai and his mother are having fun on the playground in the park. Kai went down the slide. Then, he ran through the maze. Now he is swinging on the swings.

6. In this paragraph, the word swinging means —

○ it already took place.

○ it is taking place right now.

○ it did not take place yet.

○ it will never take place.

Hint: The suffix "ing" shows that something is happening now.

GO ON

Unit 2
Core Skills Test Prep, Grade 2

OBJECTIVE 1: DETERMINING WORD MEANINGS

> Sometimes you can find out the meaning of a new word by using the words around it as clues.

Martin Luther King was a great man. He did not give up when things became <u>hard</u> for him. He did not let anyone stop him from helping others.

1. In this paragraph, the word <u>hard</u> means —

- ○ simple.
- ○ not easy.
- ○ late.
- ○ fun.

Hint: You get a clue about the word hard by reading sentences 2 and 3.

There are many kinds of sharks. Some are <u>huge</u>. The whale shark grows 60 feet long. That is more than the height of most houses. Only whales are larger.

2. In this paragraph, the word <u>huge</u> means —

- ○ big.
- ○ pretty.
- ○ small.
- ○ fast.

Hint: You get a clue about the word huge by the words "60 feet long" and by reading sentences 4 and 5.

There are many ways that fire can help us. It can keep us warm. We can cook with it. But, it can also <u>harm</u> us. It can even burn down houses.

3. In this paragraph, the word <u>harm</u> means —

- ○ help us.
- ○ warm us.
- ○ fool us.
- ○ hurt us.

Hint: You get a clue about the word harm by reading the last sentence.

GO ON

9

We have a new cat. His name is Fluffy. I want him to learn to listen to me and do what I tell him. Fluffy should learn to <u>obey</u>.

4. In this paragraph, the word <u>obey</u> means —

○ run away.

○ play.

○ follow directions.

○ be quiet.

Hint: You get a clue as to what the word <u>obey</u> means from the words "listen to me" and "do what I tell him."

Lisa loved to play baseball. She knew she could <u>strike</u> the ball with the bat when it was thrown to her. She decided to join the team.

5. In this paragraph, the word <u>strike</u> means —

○ to hit.

○ to miss.

○ to block.

○ to catch.

Hint: You get a clue as to what the word <u>strike</u> means by looking at the words "she knew she could strike the ball with the bat..."

Amy was the new girl in the class. Mira showed her where to find things around the classroom. Mira was <u>kind</u> to Amy.

6. In this paragraph, the word <u>kind</u> means —

○ helpful.

○ mean.

○ quiet.

○ lazy.

Hint: You get a clue as to what the word <u>kind</u> means by looking at what Mira did for Amy.

GO ON

10

OBJECTIVE 1: DETERMINING WORD MEANINGS

You can use the information in the passage to tell what the words mean.

Andy dug a hole and put a plant in it. Next, he filled the hole with dirt. Last, Andy watered the plant. He made sure to soak it so that it would grow.

1. In this paragraph, the word soak means —

   ○ to dry out.
   ○ to cover with dirt.
   ○ to dig deep.
   ○ to make wet.

Hint: You get a clue as to what soak means by reading the sentence before the word.

Omar knew he could have a snack when he got to the end of his homework. He did his math. Then, he did his reading. Last, he ate.

2. In this paragraph, the word end means —

   ○ start.
   ○ finish.
   ○ middle.
   ○ test.

Hint: You get a clue as to what the word end means by reading the sentences after the word.

There are many kinds of dams. A dam can be hard to build. Some are put together with dirt while others are made from rock.

3. In this paragraph, the word build means —

   ○ to sell.
   ○ to climb.
   ○ to see.
   ○ to make.

Hint: You get a clue as to what build means by reading the sentence after the word.

GO ON

11

Mandy was in a bad mood. Her mother was angry with her. Toshi called her on the telephone and told her a joke. Then Mandy started to grin.

4. In this paragraph, grin means —

- ○ cry.
- ○ see.
- ○ smile.
- ○ frown.

Hint: You get a clue about what grin means by reading the sentence before the word.

The frog leaped into the air to chase the fly. It hopped over tall grass and rocks. The frog kept leaping until it caught the fly.

5. In this paragraph, leaped means —

- ○ walked.
- ○ skipped.
- ○ jumped.
- ○ crawled.

Hint: You can get a clue about what leaped means by reading the sentences after the word.

Joy was taking a spelling test. There were two words she did not know. She wanted to quit, but she didn't. Joy kept on going.

6. In this paragraph, the word quit means —

- ○ scream.
- ○ copy.
- ○ stop.
- ○ smile.

Hint: You get a clue about what quit means by reading sentences 3 and 4.

STOP

OBJECTIVE 2: IDENTIFYING SUPPORTING IDEAS

Facts or details are important. By finding them, you will know what the passage is about.

Long ago, ships were made from logs. The center was cut out. People sat inside. They could not go very fast. These ships were also hard to make.

Things changed 5,000 years ago. They started making better ships in Egypt. These ships had sails. People could also row them. Now, they could go much faster across the water.

1. Faster boats were first built —
   ○ 5,000 years ago.
   ○ today.
   ○ from logs.
   ○ 500 years ago.

   Hint: Look at the second paragraph.

2. The first ships —
   ○ went very fast.
   ○ had sails.
   ○ could be rowed.
   ○ were hard to make.

   Hint: Read the first paragraph.

3. The ships made in Egypt were better because —
   ○ they were made from logs.
   ○ they were built 5,000 years ago.
   ○ they went faster.
   ○ their centers were cut out.

   Hint: Look at the last sentence.

GO ON

The first airplane flew on December 17, 1903. It was built by Wilbur and Orville Wright. They were brothers who had always dreamed of flying a plane.

Wilbur and Orville played with flying toys when they were young boys. Their mother made them play with their toys outside. They even wanted to fly the toys in the house.

As they grew up, they still wanted to fly. They worked very hard to build an airplane. One day it was ready. They tried to fly it on December 14. It did not work. Three days later, they were able to take off!

4. Wilbur and Orville Wright both wanted to —

- ○ stay young.
- ○ play with toys.
- ○ fly an airplane.
- ○ listen to their mother.

Hint: Look at the last sentence of the first paragraph.

5. Wilbur and Orville were —

- ○ brothers.
- ○ cousins.
- ○ friends.
- ○ uncles.

Hint: Look at the first paragraph.

6. Wilbur and Orville's airplane —

- ○ flew on December 14, 1903.
- ○ flew indoors.
- ○ was just a toy.
- ○ flew on December 17, 1903.

Hint: Read the first sentence.

GO ON

OBJECTIVE 2: IDENTIFYING SUPPORTING IDEAS

It is helpful to put events in the order they happened. This may help you to understand a passage.

Babe Ruth was a great baseball player. He was born on February 6, 1895. He had seven brothers and sisters. His mother became sick. Babe was sent away to school.

Babe learned to play baseball. He became a very good player. When he was 19 years old, Babe got money to play baseball.

Babe started out as a pitcher. He could throw the ball very hard. He could also hit the ball very far. Many teams wanted Babe to play for them.

In 1919, Babe started to play for the New York Yankees. He was a star player for over 15 years. In 1927 he set the home run record. This record was not broken until 1961. He was the star of the 1932 World Series. Babe Ruth was one of the best baseball players ever.

1. Which of these happened first in the passage?
   ○ The 1932 World Series was played.
   ○ Babe was sent away to school.
   ○ Babe Ruth was given money to play baseball.
   ○ The home run record was broken.

Hint: Look at the beginning of the passage.

>GO ON>

2. When did Babe Ruth start to play for the New York Yankees?

○ when he first learned to play baseball

○ when his mother became sick

○ in 1919

○ in 1927

Hint: Look at the last paragraph.

3. Which of these happened last in the passage?

○ Babe was a star in the World Series.

○ Babe set the home run record.

○ Many teams wanted Babe to play for them.

○ Babe's home run record was broken.

Hint: Look at the last paragraph.

OBJECTIVE 2: IDENTIFYING SUPPORTING IDEAS

Written directions tell you how to do something. Every step is important.

Did you ever make a puppet? It is a lot of fun and easy to do. There are only a few things you will need.

First, look around your house to find what you will need. Use an old sock for the body. Next, sew on buttons for the eyes. Then, glue on pieces of cloth for the mouth and ears. Last, glue yarn to the sock for hair.

1. What should you do after you find a sock?
   ○ glue on pieces of cloth for the mouth and ears
   ○ look around the house to find what you need
   ○ sew on buttons for the eyes
   ○ glue yarn to the sock for hair

   Hint: Read the third sentence of the second paragraph.

Gwen needed to pack for her trip. She wrote down all the things she would need. Next, she took out her suitcase. Gwen folded her clothes on the bed. Now she was ready to pack. When she was done, she closed the suitcase. Gwen was ready for her trip!

2. To get ready for her trip, Gwen should first —
   ○ make a list.
   ○ fold her clothes.
   ○ close her suitcase.
   ○ pack her suitcase.

   Hint: Read the passage to see what comes first.

GO ON

17

I painted my room. I wrote down the steps that I took to get the job done.

Step 1: Go to the paint store.

Step 2: Choose a color.

Step 3: Buy the paint and brushes.

Step 4: Cover things in your room. You do not want to get paint on them.

Step 5: Paint slowly. Make sure you do a careful job.

Step 6: Clean the brushes with soap and water.

Step 7: Wait for the paint to dry.

3. Which of these would you do first?

○ Clean the brushes with soap and water.

○ Buy the paint and brushes.

○ Wait for the paint to dry.

○ Cover things in your room.

Hint: Read all the steps in order.

4. When should you start to paint?

○ Step 3

○ Step 4

○ Step 5

○ Step 7

Hint: Read all the steps in order.

5. After you finish painting, you should —

○ cover things.

○ buy more paint.

○ clean the brushes.

○ go to the paint store.

Hint: Read the last two steps.

▶ GO ON ▶

18

OBJECTIVE 2: IDENTIFYING SUPPORTING IDEAS

The setting of a passage lets you know when and where the passage is taking place.

Fred Lamb had a dream to build the tallest building in the world. He wanted to put this building in New York City. Nobody had ever built such a tall building before.

All of the workers had to be very careful. They worked very hard and very long hours. They even worked at night. After six months they were done. In 1931, the Empire State Building was opened!

The Empire State Building was well built. In 1945, an airplane crashed into it. This did not knock it down.

Today, many people come to look at it. From the top, you can see for 80 miles. It is a wonderful place to visit!

1. The passage takes place in —
   ○ Fred Lamb's home.
   ○ New York City.
   ○ a dream.
   ○ an airplane.

   Hint: Read the first paragraph.

2. The Empire State Building was built —
   ○ hundreds of years ago.
   ○ last year.
   ○ in 1945.
   ○ in 1931.

   Hint: Look at the second paragraph.

3. The airplane crash took place —
   ○ before the Empire State Building was done.
   ○ while Fred Lamb was dreaming.
   ○ after the Empire State Building was built.
   ○ while the people were working at night.

   Hint: Look at the third paragraph.

▶ GO ON ▶

The first train was built in England in 1825. It did not go very fast. It could not carry many people. Sometimes it did not work at all. But it was better than riding on horses.

4. Where was the first train built?

○ the United States

○ Canada

○ England

○ Mexico

Hint: Read the first sentence.

5. When was the first train built?

○ 1825

○ 1852

○ 1895

○ 1925

Hint: Look at the first sentence.

I set up the tent in the backyard. I had my sleeping bag and my pillow. I made sure I had enough food. I took out my flashlight. It was getting dark. Before long, it was time to go to bed.

6. When is this story taking place?

○ afternoon

○ night

○ morning

○ lunch time

Hint: Look at the last two sentences.

STOP

20

OBJECTIVE 3: SUMMARIZING MAIN IDEAS

> The main idea is the meaning of a passage. Many times it is a sentence in the passage.

The earth goes around the sun. In winter, our part of the earth gets less sunshine. It is very cold and it stays darker longer. In the summer, our part of the earth gets more sunshine. Then it is very warm.

I. What is the main idea of this passage?

○ The earth moves around the sun.

○ It is cold in the winter.

○ It is darker in the winter.

○ It is warm in the summer.

Hint: What does the whole passage talk about?

Many people play soccer. It is played in every country. Soccer has been around for almost 3,000 years. Some people played soccer in China a long time ago. Then people started to play it in other countries. Soon, it was played all around the world.

2. What is the main idea of this passage?

○ Soccer has been played for almost 3,000 years.

○ Soccer is played by people all over the world.

○ Some people played soccer in China.

○ People started to play soccer in other countries.

Hint: The first two sentences and the last sentence give you the main idea.

▶ GO ON ▶

21

Hiking is a great way for you to have fun. All you need is a good pair of shoes. You can hike in many places, such as the woods or a valley. You can walk for a long or short time. Hiking is even better if you go with your friends.

3. What is the main idea of this passage?

○ You need good hiking shoes.

○ You will have a good time hiking.

○ Hikes can be long or short.

○ You can hike in the woods.

Hint: What does the whole passage talk about?

Mother's Day is a special day. There are many things you can do for your mother. You can make a pretty card or cook a nice meal. You can help clean the house or wash the clothes. It is a time to show your mother that you care.

4. What is the main idea of this passage?

○ You can cook a meal.

○ You can make a card.

○ You can help clean the house.

○ Mother's Day should be a special day.

Hint: Which choice is about the whole passage?

The winter in New York in 1994 was one to remember. There was a lot of snow. This made it hard for people to get around. Many schools were closed. It was also very cold. Many people were sick. People were glad when the winter was over.

5. What is the main idea of this passage?

○ The winter of 1994 was bad.

○ Many schools had to close.

○ People were sick.

○ It was hard to get around.

Hint: What does the whole story talk about?

GO ON

22

OBJECTIVE 3: SUMMARIZING MAIN IDEAS

A good summary contains the main idea of a passage. It is short but includes the most important points.

Bats are different from many other animals. They are the only mammal that can fly. Some bats live in trees. Most bats live in caves or in attics. They only come out at night. When they are resting, they hang upside down. Bats are very interesting animals.

1. What is this mostly about?
   ○ Most bats live in caves or attics.
   ○ Bats can fly.
   ○ Bats only come out at night.
   ○ Bats are interesting animals.

   Hint: Which sentence tells you about the whole passage?

Have you ever gone to Boston? It is a great city. There are all kinds of boats to see and walk around on. There are places to visit where you can learn about science. There are many places to get great food. Boston is a wonderful place with many things to see and do!

2. What is this mostly about?
   ○ Boston is an interesting city to visit.
   ○ You can eat good food in Boston.
   ○ Boston has all kinds of boats to see.
   ○ There are places to learn about science.

   Hint: Which sentence tells you about the whole passage?

GO ON

23

There is a lot to learn about owls. Owls are awake at night. They can see very well in the dark. They can hunt for their food. They can also hear things moving in the dark. Owls sleep during the day. They sleep high up in trees. This keeps them safe.

3. What is this passage mostly about?
   ○ There are many things to learn about owls.
   ○ Owls sleep during the day.
   ○ Owls can see in the dark.
   ○ Owls sleep high up in trees.

   Hint: Which sentence tells you about the whole passage?

Many children enjoy bowling. To play, you need to have a few things. The bowling ball has to fit your fingers. Next, you need a special pair of shoes just for bowling. Then, you are ready to bowl. Try to throw the ball straight. With some practice, you'll do fine!

4. Which sentence tells what this passage is mostly about?
   ○ The ball should be just right.
   ○ Get the right kind of shoes.
   ○ To bowl, you need some special things.
   ○ Few children enjoy bowling.

   Hint: Which sentence tells you about the whole passage?

Jane Addams was a famous woman. She wanted to help poor people. Jane bought an old house. She fixed it up. Then, she started a school for children. At night, grownups came to learn. Jane Addams worked hard to help more and more people.

5. What is this passage mostly about?
   ○ Jane Addams fixed up an old house.
   ○ Jane Addams helped many people.
   ○ Jane Addams helped teach grownups.
   ○ Jane Addams liked children.

   Hint: Which sentence tells you about the whole passage?

STOP

OBJECTIVE 4: PERCEIVING RELATIONSHIPS AND RECOGNIZING OUTCOMES

Knowing what happened (effect) and what made it happen (cause) helps you to understand what you read.

Jill could not run very fast. She could never win a race. She wanted to do better. So, every day after school she practiced running. After a while she ran faster and faster. When Jill ran in the next race, she won and was very happy!

1. Why couldn't Jill win a race at first?
- ○ She was not happy.
- ○ Jill ran in too many races.
- ○ She was not a fast runner.
- ○ Jill wanted to run fast.

Hint: Look at the first sentence.

2. Why did Jill win?
- ○ She practiced a lot.
- ○ She wanted to win.
- ○ She was very happy.
- ○ She went to school.

Hint: Look at the fourth sentence.

One day, Tony saw a beautiful plant growing in his yard. He wanted it to keep growing, so each day he watered it. He also pulled up the weeds near it. After two weeks, the plant grew even bigger. Soon, it had pretty flowers. Tony felt proud.

3. What caused the plant to grow bigger?
- ○ It was planted in Tony's yard.
- ○ It had weeds near it.
- ○ It grew pretty flowers.
- ○ Tony watered it.

Hint: What did Tony do to help the plant grow bigger?

4. Why was Tony proud?
- ○ He cared for the plant and it grew.
- ○ He saw a plant growing in the yard.
- ○ He waited for two weeks.
- ○ The flowers were pretty.

Hint: Reread the passage. Why would Tony feel proud of himself?

▶ GO ON

Long ago there lived a young woman named Margo. She lived all by herself in a house in the woods. Margo did not always like being alone. One day she found a little rabbit. The rabbit had hurt his leg. Margo felt sorry for it. She took the rabbit inside and took care of it. She gave the rabbit some lettuce to eat. The rabbit thanked Margo by licking her cheek. Margo named the rabbit Fluffy and kept it as a pet. Margo was no longer lonely.

5. Why did Margo bring the rabbit into her house?

○ She saw he was hungry.

○ She did not like to be alone.

○ She saw he was hurt.

○ She lived in the woods.

Hint: Margo brought in the rabbit. Why did she do this?

6. Why did the rabbit want to stay with Margo?

○ She took good care of him.

○ He wanted to eat more lettuce.

○ He saw Margo in the woods.

○ He did not want to be hurt.

Hint: The rabbit stayed with Margo. Why did he do this?

7. Why was Margo happy at the end of the story?

○ She did not like her house.

○ She liked to walk in the woods.

○ She wanted to find more rabbits.

○ She would not have to be alone.

Hint: Look at the last sentence. Why was Margo glad to have Fluffy?

▶GO ON▶

26

OBJECTIVE 4: PERCEIVING RELATIONSHIPS AND RECOGNIZING OUTCOMES

Sometimes you can tell what might happen next. You must think about what would make sense if the story were to go on.

Luis came home from school. His mother told him to do his homework, but he did not want to. First, he had some milk and cookies. Then, he played with his toys. After dinner he drew some pictures. Soon, it was time to go to bed.

1. What might happen to Luis the next day?
   ○ He will not have his homework.
   ○ He will do well in school.
   ○ His mother will give him toys.
   ○ He will not have milk and cookies.

Hint: What is most likely to happen the next day?

Miguel listened to the news. They said it will be very hot tomorrow. It will stay warm for the next few days. Miguel put his bathing suit on a chair. He was going to have fun.

2. What will Miguel do tomorrow?
   ○ sit on the chair
   ○ watch the news
   ○ go swimming
   ○ read a book

Hint: Read the whole paragraph.

Alicia asked to go to the bathroom. She ran down the hall. "No running in the hall," her teacher yelled. Alicia did not look where she was going. Just then, Herbie came out of his classroom. He was not looking where he was going.

3. What will happen next?
   ○ Alicia will return to her class.
   ○ Alicia and Herbie will bump into each other.
   ○ Alicia will say hello to Herbie.
   ○ Alicia's teacher will be happy.

Hint: You need to read the whole paragraph.

GO ON

Unit 2
Core Skills Test Prep, Grade 2

Chuck and Fatima wanted to put on a magic show. They practiced for a long time. They wanted to make sure they could do the tricks. When they were ready, they invited all of their friends.

4. What is probably going to happen next?

- ○ Fatima will decide not to do the tricks.
- ○ No children will come to see the show.
- ○ Chuck and Fatima will have a magic show.
- ○ Their parents will come to the show.

Hint: Think about how Chuck and Fatima got ready. What will happen next?

Kyle got a new dog named Lucky. Kyle was teaching him to chase after a ball. The first time Kyle threw it, Lucky did not chase it. The next time Kyle threw the ball, he put a treat near it. Lucky went to get it. Pretty soon he did not need the treat.

5. What will Lucky do the next time the ball is thrown?

- ○ He will go get the ball.
- ○ He will want a treat.
- ○ Lucky will run away.
- ○ Kyle will have to get it.

Hint: Read the last two sentences to find out what Lucky will do.

Alma loved to read. One day, her father gave her some books. There were books about sports. Some books were about science. Others had fairy tales and scary stories. She put them away in her closet. The next day her teacher gave her a book report to do.

6. What is Alma likely to do next?

- ○ She will clean her closet.
- ○ She will take out a book and read.
- ○ She will ask for more books.
- ○ She will not want the books.

Hint: What is in Alma's closet?

STOP

OBJECTIVE 5: MAKING INFERENCES AND GENERALIZATIONS

> The way a character acts tells you about that person's mood.

One day, Sam's parents had some news. "We are going to move to a new town! You will be going to a new school," his father said. Sam yelled, "I don't want to go. I won't have any friends!" His mother and father talked to Sam. They told him he would meet new people. He would make new friends. Now, Sam felt a little better.

1. How did Sam feel about the news?
   ○ He was mad because he did not want to move.
   ○ He felt glad because he wanted to make new friends.
   ○ He was upset because he did not like school.
   ○ He was excited about moving.

   Hint: Read what Sam said to see how he felt.

Alex lives in Florida. It is warm there most of the time. He went to visit his cousins in Maine. It was very cold and snowy. He had never seen snow before. He could not wait to play in it. After putting on some warm clothes, Alex ran outside and jumped in it. "This is great," he yelled. He laughed and kept on playing.

2. How do you think Alex felt?
   ○ angry
   ○ excited
   ○ bored
   ○ friendly

   Hint: You must read the entire passage to find out how Alex felt.

GO ON

29

Laura was working hard on her book report. She wrote her report using her best writing. Now she was ready to make the cover. Just then, her mom called her for dinner. When she was finished eating, she saw that her little brother had ripped the report. Now she would have to start over.

3. How did Laura feel when she saw what her brother had done?

○ Laura was glad.

○ Laura was angry.

○ Laura was hungry.

○ Laura was thankful.

Hint: Read the whole passage. Think about the first and last sentences.

Ari wanted to buy his mother a birthday present. He saw a necklace that he knew she would love. It cost more money than he had. Ari had a plan. Every day after school, he looked for empty soda cans. He turned them in for five cents each. Soon he had enough money to buy the necklace.

4. How will Ari feel when he goes to buy the necklace?

○ brave

○ mad

○ proud

○ silly

Hint: Read the whole paragraph. Think about what Ari was now able to do.

(STOP)

30

OBJECTIVE 6: RECOGNIZING POINTS OF VIEW, FACTS, AND OPINIONS

It is important to know the difference between fact and opinion. A fact is real and an opinion states a feeling or belief. Words that describe state opinions.

Many children are afraid of sharks. They think sharks like to eat people. Most times, this is not true. Not all sharks want to hurt people. They really want to eat tiny plants and fish. You should not be afraid of sharks.

I. Which of these is a FACT supported by information in the passage?

○ Sharks are the best fish.

○ Most sharks eat plants and fish.

○ Sharks are pretty fish.

○ You should be afraid of sharks.

Hint: Words like "best," "pretty," and "should" are opinion words.

Maine is a great place to visit. There are very nice beaches. You can swim in the ocean. You can also walk in the woods. Some people like to climb the mountains. They can climb to the top and see far away. There is a lot to do in Maine.

2. Which of these is not a fact supported by information in the passage?

○ Maine is a great place to visit.

○ You can walk in the woods.

○ Some people climb mountains.

○ There are beaches.

Hint: Facts are real and true. Which sentence is an opinion?

GO ON

Seals are in great danger. Some people hunt them for their thick fur. They use the fur to make warm coats. Other people hunt the seals for food. In some places, laws protect seals. Seals cannot be killed for any reason. We need more laws.

3. A <u>FACT</u> from the passage is that seals —

○ live in the water.

○ are in danger.

○ like to eat meat.

○ hunt people.

Hint: A fact is real and true.

Have you ever tried to high jump? High jumping can be a lot of fun. A bar rests across two poles. You have to jump over this. You run quickly up to the bar. If you jump high enough, you will go over the bar.

4. Which of these is an <u>OPINION</u>?

○ A bar rests across two poles.

○ High jumping can be a lot of fun.

○ You run quickly up to the bar.

○ You jump over the bar.

Hint: Words that describe are opinion words.

Many things happen when we eat. We chew the food into little pieces. This is so our bodies can use it. It travels down a tube into the stomach. It goes from there to other parts of the body. We all need to eat to live.

5. Which of these is a <u>FACT</u> supported by information in the passage?

○ Food travels from the stomach to the mouth.

○ We swallow big pieces of food.

○ Food is used in many parts of our body.

○ We should not eat too often.

Hint: A fact is real and true. What is really said in the passage?

32

STOP

Unit 3: Reading Comprehension

Directions: Read each passage carefully. Then read each question. Darken the circle for the correct answer, or write the answer on the lines.

Try This	More than one answer choice may seem correct. Choose the answer that goes best with the passage.

Sample A

Mr. Feld's Garden

Mr. Feld has a garden. Each day, he pulls out the weeds. He stays on his knees for a long time. Sometimes they hurt him. Today his son gave him some knee pads. Now Mr. Feld's knees won't hurt anymore.

What did Mr. Feld's son give him?
- ○ a watering can
- ○ a new rake
- ○ knee pads
- ○ some seeds

Think It Through	The correct answer is <u>knee pads</u>. The next-to-last sentence says, "Today his son gave him some knee pads."

Katie and Josephine

Katie and Josephine were waiting for the bus. They looked up at the sky. Katie put on her raincoat. Josephine pulled up her hood. The bus came. They got in fast.

1. What were the girls doing?
- ○ playing football
- ○ waiting for the bus
- ○ waiting for the train
- ○ riding an airplane

2. Why did Katie and Josephine get into the bus fast?

_____

_____

Unit 3
Core Skills Test Prep, Grade 2

The Lion and the Mouse

A big, fierce lion was sleeping under a tree. A mouse ran up on the lion's back. Then the lion woke up, and he was angry at the mouse. He caught the mouse in his paw.

"Please do not eat me," said the mouse. "If you let me go, I will help you some time."

The lion thought the mouse was funny. "How could you help me?" he laughed. But then he let the mouse go.

Later that day the lion got caught in a hunter's net. He tried and tried to get free, but he could not get out of the net. The lion was ready to give up, but then he saw the mouse.

"Please help me," the lion said. The mouse began to chew on the net. Soon the net broke apart, and the lion was able to climb out of the net. The mouse had set the lion free.

3. How did the mouse help the lion?

○ She brought the lion food.

○ She found the lion's friends.

○ She fixed the lion's paw.

○ She chewed the net apart.

4. The boxes below show things that happened in the story.

The lion caught the mouse.		The mouse set the lion free.
I	2	3

What belongs in Box 2?

○ The lion was sleeping.

○ The mouse woke up the lion.

○ The lion let the mouse go.

○ The mouse ran up the lion's back.

5. Why was the lion angry?

_____

_____

_____

6. Which of these lessons best fits the story?

○ Little friends cannot help.

○ A mouse should not walk on a lion.

○ Little friends can be good friends.

○ Laughing makes you feel better.

▶ GO ON ▶

34

A Letter to Harry

Dear Harry,

I wish you lived near me. We had the best costume party last night. It would have been more fun if you had been here. I dressed up like a cat. We invited all the kids on my street. Some of my friends from school came, too.

We had the party in the garage. I helped my dad fix it up. We hung colorful banners and streamers from the ceiling. My dad dressed up like a monster. We bobbed for apples in a big pail of water. The only way I could get one was to put my whole head under the water. I pushed the apple against the bottom of the pail and finally got it.

Later my dad made some special root beer. This is how he did it:

First, he put sugar into some water, and then he added root beer *extract.* That's the flavoring that makes it taste like root beer.

To finish, my dad stirred it and added lots of dry ice. When he poured in the dry ice, it made a lot of white smoke!

Chris had one of the best costumes. He was dressed like a hot dog. At the end of the party we helped Mom make popcorn.

What have you been doing? When are you going to come and visit? My mom says you can come anytime. We're going to Texas for New Year's Day. Write me soon.

Your friend,
Tom

GO ON

35

7. What is Tom's letter mostly about?

- ○ his party
- ○ his class at school
- ○ his costume
- ○ his trip to Texas

8. How does Tom feel about Harry?

_____

_____

_____

9. If you are making root beer, you should —

- ○ add sugar to flour.
- ○ stir in butter.
- ○ pour in milk.
- ○ add sugar to water.

10. What kind of party did Tom have?

- ○ a pizza party
- ○ a birthday party
- ○ a garden party
- ○ a costume party

11. In this story, Harry is the name of Tom's —

- ○ friend.
- ○ teacher.
- ○ uncle.
- ○ neighbor.

12. In this story, what does the word *extract* mean?

- ○ a kind of sugar
- ○ a kind of flavoring
- ○ a kind of nut
- ○ a kind of flour

13. When did Tom write the letter?

- ○ on a Monday
- ○ during the summer
- ○ the day after his party
- ○ on New Year's Day

14. Tom's letter does not tell —

- ○ where his friend Harry lives.
- ○ what costume his dad wore.
- ○ about bobbing for apples.
- ○ where he is going for New Year's Day.

▶GO ON▶

36

Join Now!

This month is the time to join in and help others. Any second grader at Smith School can join in.

Read the list of things to do. Choose those you like best. Sign up on the sheet below by Thursday.

Ms. Salina will lead the activities. Students who do two or more things from the list this month will earn a volunteer pin.

To help others, we will:

1. Read to younger students.
2. Pick up litter at Travis Park.
3. Make greeting cards to send to a hospital.
4. Record songs on tape to send to a nursing home.

Your Name	Activity Numbers	Your Teacher's Name
Meg Klein	2,4	Mr. Ward

15. Who will earn a pin?

- ○ all students who sign up
- ○ Ms. Salina's homeroom students
- ○ students who do at least two things from the list
- ○ students in the hospital

16. Why would students volunteer?

_____

_____

17. After students sign up, what will probably happen next?

- ○ Ms. Salina will speak to them.
- ○ They will sing songs.
- ○ They will get a volunteer pin.
- ○ They will go shopping.

18. Which of the following is <u>not</u> listed on the sign-up sheet?

- ○ your name
- ○ your room number
- ○ activity numbers
- ○ your teacher's name

▶GO ON◀

A Great Play

Dawn had a part in the school play. She had to wear a costume. First, she put on a gray suit with a long tail. Then, she painted a pink circle on her nose. A pair of big gray ears finished the costume. It was time for her part. She walked onto the stage. A boy dressed like a cat crawled toward her. She grabbed a piece of cheese and ran. She was faster than the cat. Everyone laughed and laughed.

19. Why did Dawn wear a costume?
- ○ She was going to a party.
- ○ She was playing with friends.
- ○ She was in a school play.
- ○ She liked to dress up.

20. What animal was Dawn most likely dressed as?
- ○ an elephant
- ○ a dog
- ○ a cat
- ○ a mouse

21. What is this story mostly about?
- ○ Dawn's part in the school play
- ○ how to make costumes for plays
- ○ how to act in plays
- ○ animals in plays

22. What could be another title for this story?

_____

_____

STOP

Name _____ Date _____

TEST

Sample A

A Note for Ellen

Ellen's mother was going to be home late. She left a note for Ellen that said, "Please clean your room. Then you may read or watch television. I should be home about 4:00."

What should Ellen do first?

○ clean her room
○ watch television
○ read
○ call her friends

Growing Flowers

To grow flowers, do the following:
1. Put dirt in a pot.
2. Place flower seeds in the pot.
3. Cover the seeds with more dirt.
4. Put the pot in the sun.
5. Water the seeds, and wait for the flowers to grow!

I. What is the last thing you should do?

○ cover the seeds with dirt
○ put dirt in the pot
○ buy seeds
○ water the seeds

2. What is the best way to find out more about growing flowers?

○ Read a book about gardening.
○ Put cut flowers in a vase.
○ Draw pictures of flowers.
○ Sit in the sun.

3. To grow flowers you will need —

○ a shovel.
○ seeds.
○ gloves.
○ a spoon.

4. Where should you put the pot?

_____

_____

_____

▶ **GO ON** ➡

All About Owls

Did you know that owls are good hunters? Owls sleep all day long. At night they wake up and fly around. They look for mice to eat. Owls have very big eyes. Big eyes let in more light. Owls can see better at night than we can. Owls also hear very well. They can hear a mouse running in the grass. They can fly without making any noise at all. All these things make owls good hunters.

5. This passage does <u>not</u> tell —
- ○ the kind of eyes owls have.
- ○ what makes owls good hunters.
- ○ about different kinds of owls.
- ○ what owls like to eat.

6. This passage was written mainly to —
- ○ ask you to join a club.
- ○ explain how important sleep is for good health.
- ○ tell about a kind of bird.
- ○ describe what animals do at night.

7. A special thing about the owl is that it can fly very —
- ○ quietly.   ○ loudly.
- ○ quickly.   ○ high in the air.

8. Why can owls see better at night?

_____

_____

9. When do owls sleep?
- ○ at night
- ○ during the afternoon
- ○ through the morning
- ○ all day

▶ GO ON ▶

40

A Scary Walk

"What a great day for a walk!" John said. He could hear the birds singing. John was glad that he had made this trip to the mountains. After breakfast John took off, whistling a tune. The trail went up the mountain. He walked for a while, and then he looked for a rock to rest on. John was tired. "What a mountain man I turned out to be!" he said.

While he rested, John looked around. Suddenly he saw the opening to a cave. It was big enough to walk through. "I wonder how deep it is," he said. "I wonder if there are any cave drawings! I guess the only way to find out is to see for myself."

At first John had no trouble seeing in the cave. He went around a bend. He lit a match. "Just a little farther," he said to himself. Suddenly his match went out! He lit another one. But now things looked strange. John was lost!

When his second match went out, John got really frightened. Then he thought he heard a scratching noise. John struck his last match. In the light he saw hundreds of bats hanging on the cave walls! Their eyes glittered red. John started screaming and running as fast as he could. Luckily for John, he was running in the right direction. He ran all the way back to his camp.

Core Skills Test Prep, Grade 2

GO ON

10. What did John hear when he started his walk?

- ○ water running
- ○ bats scratching
- ○ dogs barking
- ○ birds singing

11. What will John probably do next?

_____

_____

_____

12. What is this story mostly about?

- ○ bats hanging on cave walls
- ○ John's adventure in a cave
- ○ using matches wisely
- ○ hiking safety

13. Why did John go into the cave?

- ○ He liked caves.
- ○ He wanted to see what was inside the cave.
- ○ He was looking for a friend.
- ○ It started to rain.

14. These boxes show things that happened in the story.

John rested on a rock.		John saw hundreds of bats.
1	2	3

What belongs in Box 2?

- ○ John ran back to camp.
- ○ John walked up the mountain.
- ○ John got lost in a cave.
- ○ John ate breakfast.

15. How did John feel when he saw the bats?

- ○ interested
- ○ angry
- ○ frightened
- ○ sad

16. This story is most like a —

- ○ poem.
- ○ true story.
- ○ fairy tale.
- ○ tall tale.

17. Another name for this story is —

- ○ "Mountain Man"
- ○ "Finding Cave Drawings"
- ○ "John's Surprise"
- ○ "How to Explore Caves"

STOP

Unit 4: Reading Vocabulary

UNDERSTANDING WORD MEANINGS

Directions: Darken the circle for the word or words that have the <u>same</u> or almost the <u>same</u> meaning as the underlined word.

Try This	Choose your answer carefully. Some choices may seem correct. Be sure to think about the meaning of the underlined word.

Sample A

To <u>raise</u> something is to —

○ lift it.   ○ fly it.

○ count it.   ○ open it.

Think It Through	The correct answer is <u>lift</u> it. If you raise something, you lift it up. To raise something is not to count it, fly it, or open it.

STOP

1. To <u>choose</u> is to —

   ○ hide.   ○ color.

   ○ check.   ○ pick.

2. A <u>blizzard</u> is most like a —

   ○ thunderstorm.

   ○ snowstorm.

   ○ river.

   ○ movie.

3. To <u>shout</u> is to —

   ○ jump.

   ○ slip.

   ○ yell.

   ○ skip.

4. <u>Least</u> means —

   ○ best.   ○ smallest.

   ○ closest.   ○ fastest.

5. A <u>pail</u> is most like a —

   ○ bucket.   ○ house.

   ○ pain.   ○ hill.

6. Something that is moving <u>forward</u> is going —

   ○ back.

   ○ ahead.

   ○ behind.

   ○ over.

STOP

MATCHING WORDS WITH MORE THAN ONE MEANING

Directions: Darken the circle beside the sentence that uses the underlined word in the same way as the sentence in the box, or write the answer on the blank lines.

Try This	Read the sentence in the box. Decide what the underlined word means. Then find the sentence with the underlined word that has the same meaning.

Sample A

> Have you ever seen a two-dollar <u>bill</u>?

In which sentence does <u>bill</u> mean the same as it does in the sentence above?

○ I paid with two quarters and one dollar <u>bill</u>.

○ Uncle Carl got a <u>bill</u> for the newspaper.

○ A parrot has a big <u>bill</u>.

○ The store will <u>bill</u> us for these shoes.

Think It Through	The correct answer is the <u>first sentence</u>, <u>I paid with two quarters and one dollar bill</u>. In this sentence and the sentence in the box, <u>bill</u> means "a type of money."

🛑 STOP

1.

> The sun's <u>light</u> is bright.

In which sentence does <u>light</u> mean the same as it does in the sentence above?

○ Will you <u>light</u> the candles?

○ The <u>light</u> from the flashlight helped us to see.

○ That bag is <u>light</u>, not heavy.

○ Pink is a <u>light</u> color.

2.

> It is Tia's turn to <u>ring</u> the bell.

Use <u>ring</u> in a sentence. It should have the same meaning as it does in the sentence in the box.

_____

_____

🛑 STOP

44

USING CONTEXT CLUES

Directions: Darken the circle for the word or words that give the meaning of the underlined word, or write the answer on the blank lines.

Try This	Read the first sentence carefully. Look for clue words in the sentence to help you. Then use each answer choice in place of the underlined word. Remember that the underlined word and your answer must have the same meaning.

Sample A

The magician made the rabbit vanish from our sight. <u>Vanish</u> means —

○ jump.   ○ disappear.

○ shine.   ○ smile.

Think It Through	The correct answer is disappear. Vanish means to no longer be seen. All four choices are things a magician could make a rabbit do. But only disappear has the same meaning as vanish.

---

1. Singing, talking loudly, or whistling is <u>forbidden</u> in the library. What does <u>forbidden</u> mean?

   _____

   _____

2. The artist made a quick pencil <u>sketch</u> of the village. <u>Sketch</u> means —

   ○ drawing.   ○ song.

   ○ story.   ○ fence.

3. Melissa plans to <u>save</u> money so she will be able to buy some new skates. <u>Save</u> means —

   ○ keep.

   ○ bet.

   ○ pay.

   ○ find.

4. He <u>shoved</u> the frightened actor onto the stage. <u>Shoved</u> means —

   ○ sang.

   ○ returned.

   ○ pushed.

   ○ read.

STOP

RECOGNIZING COMPOUND WORDS

Directions: Darken the circle under the compound word.

Try This	Look carefully at each word. Then look for the word that is made up of two words put together.

Sample A

carrot ○   harbor ○   herself ○

Think It Through	Herself is a compound word made up of the words her and self. Each of these words can stand alone. Harbor and carrot are not made up of two words put together.

STOP

1. mailbox ○   listen ○   drawing ○

5. anyway ○   making ○   after ○

2. closet ○   airplane ○   fasten ○

6. inches ○   someone ○   teacher ○

3. football ○   looked ○   backing ○

7. fiddle ○   rather ○   bedroom ○

4. pencil ○   follow ○   outside ○

8. bottle ○   bluebird ○   hundred ○

STOP

46

CHOOSING CORRECT WORDS

Directions: Darken the circle under the word you hear.

Try This	Listen to the whole word. Then say the word to yourself. Notice that the answer choices are almost the same, but each word has a different ending. Choose your answer carefully.

Sample A

jumps	jumping	jumped
○	○	○

Think It Through	The correct answer is the third word, <u>jumped</u>. Although the word <u>jump</u> is a part of each word, <u>jumped</u> is the word that you heard.

(STOP)

I.	painting ○	paints ○	painter ○	5.	read ○	reading ○	reader ○
2.	quit ○	quitting ○	quits ○	6.	sweets ○	sweeter ○	sweetest ○
3.	care ○	careless ○	careful ○	7.	hardly ○	hardest ○	harder ○
4.	nearly ○	nearest ○	nearer ○	8.	nicest ○	nicely ○	nicer ○

(STOP)

47

RECOGNIZING CONTRACTIONS

Directions: Darken the circle under the contraction that means the same as the two words you hear.

Try This	Study the three contractions carefully. Then silently say the two words that form each contraction. The answer choices may look alike, but only one has the same meaning as the two words that you hear.

Sample A

haven't   hadn't   hasn't
○   ○   ○

Think It Through	The correct answer is the first word, <u>haven't</u>. The contraction <u>haven't</u> means <u>have not</u>. The sentence "I have not gone there" has the same meaning as the sentence "I haven't gone there." <u>Hadn't</u> means <u>had not</u>, and <u>hasn't</u> means <u>has not</u>.

STOP

1. we'll   we've   we're
    ○   ○   ○

5. who's   who'll   who'd
    ○   ○   ○

2. weren't   won't   wasn't
    ○   ○   ○

6. he'd   he'll   he's
    ○   ○   ○

3. don't   didn't   doesn't
    ○   ○   ○

7. he's   he'll   he'd
    ○   ○   ○

4. they'd   they're   they'll
    ○   ○   ○

8. you're   you've   you'd
    ○   ○   ○

STOP

MATCHING WORD SOUNDS

Directions: Darken the circle under the word that has the same sound or sounds as the underlined part of the first word in each row.

Try This	Say the first word to yourself. Decide how the underlined part of the word sounds. Then as you say each answer choice, listen for that sound.

Sample A

n<u>o</u>se

low   night   loop
○   ○   ○

Think It Through	<u>Low</u> is the correct answer. The "o" in <u>low</u> makes the same sound as the "o" in <u>nose</u>.

STOP

---

1. <u>th</u>ere

     this   think   thin
     ○   ○   ○

2. l<u>ou</u>d

     through   lid   cow
     ○   ○   ○

3. but<u>t</u>er

     mother   bunny   writing
     ○   ○   ○

4. quil<u>t</u>

     mall   wilt   queen
     ○   ○   ○

5. c<u>u</u>te

     pulling   luck   noon
     ○   ○   ○

6. <u>r</u>are

     rain   fair   rough
     ○   ○   ○

7. <u>c</u>at

     city   kitten   hat
     ○   ○   ○

8. <u>s</u>tep

     desk   fast   teach
     ○   ○   ○

STOP

TEST

Sample A

A <u>command</u> is a kind of —

- ○ order.
- ○ boat.
- ○ test.
- ○ question.

STOP

1. <u>Hardly</u> means —
   - ○ a lot.
   - ○ not at all.
   - ○ more than.
   - ○ barely.

2. To <u>begin</u> is to —
   - ○ start.
   - ○ end.
   - ○ laugh.
   - ○ think.

3. A <u>bundle</u> is a —
   - ○ supper.
   - ○ mitten.
   - ○ bunch.
   - ○ bread.

4. If something <u>sparkles</u>, it —
   - ○ shines.
   - ○ bothers.
   - ○ pays.
   - ○ wins.

Sample B

> What <u>time</u> does the show start?

In which sentence does <u>time</u> mean the same as it does in the sentence above?

- ○ I will <u>time</u> my brother's race.
- ○ We kept <u>time</u> with the music.
- ○ Everyone had a good <u>time</u>.
- ○ It's <u>time</u> for lunch.

STOP

5.
> Did you feel a <u>drop</u> of rain?

In which sentence does <u>drop</u> mean the same as it does in the sentence above?

- ○ I put the letter in the mail <u>drop</u>.
- ○ Please wipe up the <u>drop</u> of paint.
- ○ Leon's mom will <u>drop</u> us off.
- ○ Don't <u>drop</u> that glass!

6.
> I tied <u>string</u> to my kite.

In which sentence does <u>string</u> mean the same as it does in the sentence above?

- ○ Maribel wore a <u>string</u> of beads.
- ○ The box was tied with <u>string</u>.
- ○ His violin needs a new <u>string</u>.
- ○ We will <u>string</u> these lights.

GO ON

7.

> Exercise is the <u>key</u> to good health.

In which sentence does <u>key</u> mean the same as it does in the sentence above?

○ A <u>key</u> on the piano is stuck.

○ I lost my <u>key</u> to the front door.

○ In what <u>key</u> are you singing?

○ Tim found the <u>key</u> to solving the puzzle.

8.

> We planted flowers <u>last</u> spring.

Write a sentence in which <u>last</u> means the same as it does in the sentence above.

_____

_____

9.

> Did you find the <u>iron</u> pot?

In which sentence does <u>iron</u> mean the same as it does in the sentence above?

○ The <u>iron</u> horseshoe is strong.

○ Lisa needs to <u>iron</u> her dress.

○ <u>Iron</u> out your differences.

○ Did you plug in the <u>iron</u>?

Sample C

The two people yelling <u>argue</u> about everything. To <u>argue</u> means to —

○ fight.   ○ sing.

○ plan.   ○ read.

10. We made a star <u>pattern</u> with beads. <u>Pattern</u> means —

○ circle.

○ design.

○ necklace.

○ string.

11. A family finally moved into the house that had been <u>vacant</u> for months. <u>Vacant</u> means —

○ white.

○ empty.

○ burned.

○ filled.

12. He painted <u>bold</u> colors next to soft ones. <u>Bold</u> means —

○ dull.

○ bright.

○ mixed.

○ quiet.

STOP

Name _____ Date _____

Sample A

postcard   eleven   pilot
  ◯   ◯   ◯

STOP

_____

1. frying   mitten   raincoat
  ◯   ◯   ◯

2. notebook   other   parent
  ◯   ◯   ◯

3. fresher   bathtub   bottle
  ◯   ◯   ◯

4. wisdom   upstairs   artist
  ◯   ◯   ◯

5. finger   grassy   birthday
  ◯   ◯   ◯

6. remain   sidewalk   happen
  ◯   ◯   ◯

Sample B

neatly   neatest   neater
  ◯   ◯   ◯

STOP

_____

7. slower   slowly   slowest
  ◯   ◯   ◯

8. calls   called   calling
  ◯   ◯   ◯

9. helper   helps   helping
  ◯   ◯   ◯

10. folds   folded   folding
  ◯   ◯   ◯

11. clearer   clearly   clearest
  ◯   ◯   ◯

12. locks   locked   locking
  ◯   ◯   ◯

GO ON

Sample C

we've	we're	we'd
○	○	○

STOP

_____

13.

it's	it'll	it'd
○	○	○

14.

hadn't	hasn't	haven't
○	○	○

15.

you'd	you'll	you've
○	○	○

16.

wouldn't	couldn't	shouldn't
○	○	○

17.

what's	where's	that's
○	○	○

18.

I'll	I'd	I've
○	○	○

Sample D

wish

shop	print	desk
○	○	○

STOP

_____

19. reach

shore	rink	chip
○	○	○

20. center

crate	loose	inch
○	○	○

21. pine

pitch	peach	tie
○	○	○

22. pie

fine	car	mop
○	○	○

23. flat

flew	apple	west
○	○	○

24. roast

grow	spoon	ripe
○	○	○

STOP

Unit 5: Math Problem-Solving Strategies

OVERVIEW
The Problem-Solving Plan

Here are the steps to solve problems:

STEP 1: **WHAT IS THE QUESTION?**
Read the problem. Can you see what you must find? What is the question?

STEP 2: **FIND THE FACTS**
Find the facts:
    A. IMPORTANT FACTS...You need these to solve the problem.
    B. FACTS YOU DON'T NEED...Some facts are not needed to solve the problem.
    C. MORE FACTS NEEDED...Do you need more facts to solve the problem?

STEP 3: **CHOOSE A WAY TO SOLVE**
Plan a way to solve the problem.

STEP 4: **SOLVE**
Use your plan to solve the problem.

STEP 5: **DOES YOUR RESPONSE MAKE SENSE?**
Write your answer in a complete sentence.
Read the problem again.
Does your answer make sense?

PROBLEM 1

PROBLEM/QUESTION:

A store sells apples. The first apple costs 25¢. Each apple after that costs 20¢. If Paul buys 3 apples, how much does he pay?

STEP 1: WHAT IS THE QUESTION/GOAL?

STEP 2: FIND THE FACTS

STEP 3: SELECT A STRATEGY

STEP 4: SOLVE

STEP 5: DOES YOUR RESPONSE MAKE SENSE?

PROBLEM 2

PROBLEM/QUESTION:

Jenny said, "I am thinking of a number. The number is less than 9 and greater than 5. It is an odd number." Name the number.

STEP 1: WHAT IS THE QUESTION/GOAL?

STEP 2: FIND THE FACTS

STEP 3: SELECT A STRATEGY

STEP 4: SOLVE

STEP 5: DOES YOUR RESPONSE MAKE SENSE?

Name _____ Date _____

Unit 6: Math Problem Solving

UNDERSTANDING NUMERATION

Directions: Darken the circle for the correct answer, or write the answer on the lines.

Try This	Listen carefully to the question your teacher reads. Be sure to think about which numbers stand for ones, tens, hundreds, and so on.

Sample A

300 + 50

300	3,050	350	30,050
○	○	○	○

Think It Through	The correct answer is <u>350</u>. This is the only number that equals 300 + 50.

STOP

_____

1. 903

_____

_____

2.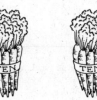

    9   5   3   6

   ○   ○   ○   ○

3.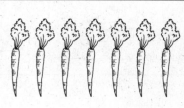

75	57	67	58
○	○	○	○

STOP

USING WHOLE NUMBERS, FRACTIONS, AND DECIMALS

Directions: Darken the circle for the correct answer, or write the answer on the lines.

Try This	Look at each picture or number sentence for the problem. Think carefully about the information in the problem. Then find the picture or number that answers the question.

Sample A

  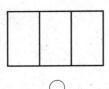

○   ○   ○   ○

Think It Through	The correct answer is the <u>third</u> shape. All the other shapes are divided into fourths.

_____ **STOP**

1.

○ $6 + 2 = 8$ ○ $10 - 2 = 8$

○ $6 - 2 = 4$ ○ $8 + 2 = 10$

2.

○   ○   ○   ○

3.

| $8 + \square = 8$ |

_____

4.

| $18 + \square = 21 + 18$ |

39   21   18   3
○   ○   ○   ○   **STOP**

WORKING WITH PATTERNS AND RELATIONSHIPS

Directions: Darken the circle for the correct answer, or write the answer on the lines.

Try This	Listen carefully to each problem. Study the pictures or numbers that you see. Then find the correct answer.

Sample A

25   17   15   11
○   ○   ○   ○

Think It Through	The correct answer is 15. Each of the numbers is 3 greater than the one before it. 12 + 3 = 15, so this is the missing number.

STOP

1.

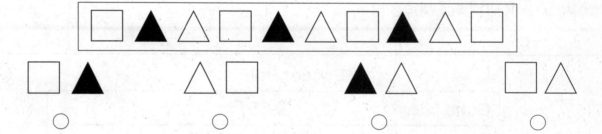

○   ○   ○   ○

2.

10	15	20		30

_____

_____

3.

62 63 64   ○   ○   ○   ○

STOP

WORKING WITH STATISTICS AND PROBABILITY

Directions: Darken the circle for the correct answer, or write the answer on the lines.

| **Try This** | Look carefully at the picture, graph, or chart. Think about the information in the problem. Then find the picture or number that answers the problem. |

Sample A

| Sand dollar | Conch | Whelk | Scallop |
| ꟷꟷꟷꟷ /// | //// | ꟷꟷꟷꟷ / | /// |

Sand dollar ○   **Conch** ○   **Whelk** ○   **Scallop** ○

| **Think It Through** | The correct answer is the <u>whelk</u>. If you count the tally marks, Ann found six whelk shells. |

STOP

I.

Soccer Points

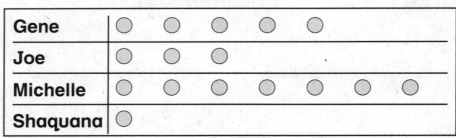

Gene	○ ○ ○ ○ ○
Joe	○ ○ ○
Michelle	○ ○ ○ ○ ○ ○ ○
Shaquana	○

Each ○ = I point

2.

    △   ○   □

      ○   ○   ○   ○

STOP

Unit 6
Core Skills Test Prep, Grade 2

WORKING WITH GEOMETRY

Directions: Darken the circle for the correct answer.

Try This	Listen carefully to the questions. Use the pictures you see to help you answer the questions.

Sample A

 ○   ○   ○   ○

Think It Through	The correct answer is the <u>third</u> figure. If you fold this figure on the dotted line, each side will be the same.

STOP

I.

 ○    ○    ○    ○

2.

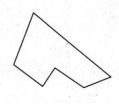 | 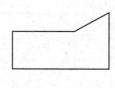 ○   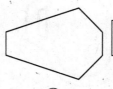 ○   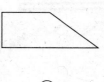 ○    ○

3.

 |  ○    ○    ○    ○

STOP

WORKING WITH MEASUREMENT

Directions: Darken the circle for the correct answer, or write the answer on the lines.

| **Try This** | Look at each picture or number for the problem. Think about what the question is asking. Then find the information to help you answer the question. |

Sample A

   3¢   5¢   10¢   15¢
   ○   ○   ○   ○

| **Think It Through** | The correct answer is <u>15¢</u>. Sue has 28¢. The banana costs 13¢. To find out how much Sue gets back, subtract 13¢ from 28¢. This gives you the answer, 15¢. |

STOP

1.

_____

_____

2.   Kilometers   Pounds   Inches   Grams
       ○   ○   ○   ○

3.

○ Monday   ○ Friday

○ Tuesday   ○ Saturday

STOP

SOLVING PROBLEMS

Directions: Darken the circle for the correct answer, or write the answer on the lines.

Try This	Look at each number or number sentence for the problem. Think carefully about the information in the problem. Then decide what you should do to find the answer.

Sample A

○ $12 + 8 = \square$ ○ $12 + 4 = \square$

○ $12 - 8 = \square$ ○ $12 - \square = 6$

Think It Through	The correct answer is <u>12 − 8</u>. The clue words, "has left," tell you to subtract. Mrs. Chong has 12 flowers and puts 8 in a vase, so 12 − 8 is the number sentence that answers the question.

STOP

1.

○ $9 - 3 = \square$ ○ $3 + 9 = \square$

○ $12 - 9 = \square$ ○ $3 + \square = 9$

2.

38   34   29   24
○   ○   ○   ○

3.

_____

_____

4.

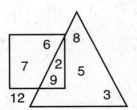

2   5   6   8
○   ○   ○   ○

STOP

MATH PROCEDURES

UNDERSTANDING COMPUTATION

Directions: Darken the circle for the correct answer. If the correct answer is not given, darken the circle for <u>NH</u> for <u>Not Here</u>. If there are no choices, write the answer on the blank lines.

Try This	Listen to the question. Think about what the question is asking. Write down on scratch paper the numbers given in the problem. Then decide how to solve the problem.

Sample A

9   5

4   8   14   16   NH
○   ○   ○   ○   ○

Think It Through	The correct answer is the third answer choice, <u>14</u>. She gets 9 presents from her friends and 5 from her family. The word altogether tells you to add. So there are <u>14</u> presents <u>altogether</u>, because $9 + 5 = $ <u>14</u>.

STOP

1.

60   34

104   94   44   34   NH
○   ○   ○   ○   ○

2.

5   3

8   7   3   2   NH
○   ○   ○   ○   ○

3.

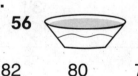

56   24

82   80   70   32   NH
○   ○   ○   ○   ○

4.

18   7

_____

_____

GO ON

64

5.

 55   23

18 ○   22 ○   32 ○   78 ○   NH ○

6.

 26   9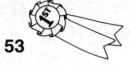

15 ○   17 ○   27 ○   35 ○   NH ○

7.

 53   23

40 ○   33 ○   23 ○   20 ○   NH ○

8.

123   47

85 ○   83 ○   76 ○   74 ○   NH ○

9.

41   12

29 ○   39 ○   53 ○   63 ○   NH ○

10.

 12   9

21 ○   13 ○   11 ○   3 ○   NH ○

11.

 207   66

373 ○   301 ○   141 ○   140 ○   NH ○

12.

 82   47

139 ○   129 ○   45 ○   35 ○   NH ○

13.

126   71

_____

_____

14.

30   16

46 ○   24 ○   14 ○   6 ○   NH ○

Core Skills Test Prep, Grade 2

STOP

USING COMPUTATION

Directions: Darken the circle for the correct answer. If the correct answer is not given, darken the circle for <u>NH</u> for <u>Not Here</u>. If there are no circles, write the answer on the lines.

Try This	Study the problem carefully. Decide if you need to add or subtract. Then work the problem on scratch paper.

Sample A

$$17$$
$$-\ 9$$

6   8   26   28   NH
○   ○   ○   ○   ○

Think It Through	The correct answer is <u>8</u>. $17 - 9 = 8$. The second answer choice is correct because you can check your answer by adding the 9 and the 8, which gives you 17.

(STOP)

1.
$$410$$
$$+\ 62$$

482   472   358   348   NH
○   ○   ○   ○   ○

---

2. $13 - 8 = \square$

8   7   6   5   NH
○   ○   ○   ○   ○

---

3. $5 + 2 + 9 = \square$

17   16   15   14   NH
○   ○   ○   ○   ○

4. $24 + 13 = \square$

11   21   37   47   NH
○   ○   ○   ○   ○

---

5. $8 + 7 = \square$

1   14   16   25   NH
○   ○   ○   ○   ○

6.
$$51$$
$$-\ 17$$

_____

_____

_____

(STOP)

TEST 1: MATH PROBLEM SOLVING

Sample A

- ○ 5 − 2 = 3   ○ 5 + 1 = 6
- ○ 4 − 1 = 3   ○ 5 − 1 = 4

STOP

1.

72		95

43   71   89   96
○   ○   ○   ○

2.

294 | 0   2   4   9
    ○   ○   ○   ○

3.

156   198   220   314
○   ○   ○   ○

4.

60,092   6,092   6,902   692
○   ○   ○   ○

5.

538 | _____

      _____

GO ON

6.

(65) (70) (75) ( ) (85)

7.

$23 + 17 = \square + 23$

    6   17   32   40

    ○   ○   ○   ○

8.

13 14 15   ○   ○ ○   ○

9.

   $\frac{1}{2}$ $\frac{1}{3}$ $\frac{1}{4}$ $\frac{2}{1}$

   ○   ○   ○   ○

10.

   ○   ○   ○   ○

GO ON

11.

Name	Height
Jimmy	45 in.
Ming	48 in.
Ralph	52 in.
Anna	60 in.

Jimmy	Ming	Ralph	Anna
◯	◯	◯	◯

12.

      ____

◯   ◯   ◯   ◯

Animal Tracks

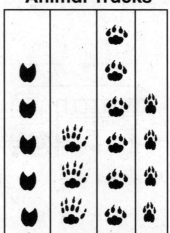

Deer Raccoon Fox Rabbit

Each track = 1 animal

13.

Deer	Raccoon	Fox	Rabbit
◯	◯	◯	◯

14. _____

_____

GO ON ▶

15.

_____

_____

16.

◯   ◯   ◯   ◯

17.

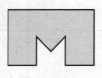

◯   ◯   ◯   ◯

18.

7   4   3   2

◯   ◯   ◯   ◯

19.

A   B   C   D

◯   ◯   ◯   ◯

20.

  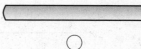

◯   ◯   ◯   ◯

GO ON

Unit 6
Core Skills Test Prep, Grade 2

21.

| 30¢ | 15¢ | 11¢ | 6¢ |
| ○ | ○ | ○ | ○ |

22.

_____

_____

23.

| Pounds | Teaspoons | Inches | Ounces |
| ○ | ○ | ○ | ○ |

24.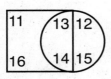

| 16 | 15 | 13 | 11 |
| ○ | ○ | ○ | ○ |

25.

| 24 | 26 | 28 | 29 |
| ○ | ○ | ○ | ○ |

26.

○ 16 − 5 = □   ○ 16 + 5 = □

○ 16 − □ = 5   ○ 5 + □ = 16

STOP

Name _____ Date _____

TEST 2: MATH PROCEDURES

Sample A

146 **42**

94	104	188	198	NH
○	○	○	○	○

 STOP

Sample B

46 **25**

21	31	61	71	NH
○	○	○	○	○

1.

13 **6**

6	7	9	29	NH
○	○	○	○	○

2.

27 **8**

_____

3.

8 **3**

4	6	11	15	NH
○	○	○	○	○

4.

9 **4**

13	7	6	4	NH
○	○	○	○	○

5.

32 **16**

16	26	48	58	NH
○	○	○	○	○

6. $7 + 5 = \square$

12	11	3	2	NH
○	○	○	○	○

7.

80 **67**

147	137	27	17	NH
○	○	○	○	○

8.

614 **44**

1,054	1,008	658	638	NH
○	○	○	○	○

GO ON

Unit 6
Core Skills Test Prep, Grade 2

9.
$$\begin{array}{r} 14 \\ -\ 8 \\ \hline \end{array}$$

22	12	7	6	NH
○	○	○	○	○

10.   39 + 20 = ☐

69	59	29	19	NH
○	○	○	○	○

11.
$$\begin{array}{r} 76 \\ +\ 8 \\ \hline \end{array}$$

68	74	78	84	NH
○	○	○	○	○

12.
$$\begin{array}{r} 25 \\ 10 \\ +\ 13 \\ \hline \end{array}$$

58	52	48	38	NH
○	○	○	○	○

13.
$$\begin{array}{r} 61 \\ -\ 35 \\ \hline \end{array}$$

26	36	86	96	NH
○	○	○	○	○

14.
$$\begin{array}{r} 417 \\ -\ 12 \\ \hline \end{array}$$

439	429	425	405	NH
○	○	○	○	○

15.   9 + ☐ = 12

2	3	4	5	NH
○	○	○	○	○

16.
$$\begin{array}{r} 45 \\ -\ 8 \\ \hline \end{array}$$

_____

_____

17.
$$\begin{array}{r} 515 \\ +\ 46 \\ \hline \end{array}$$

561	551	461	451	NH
○	○	○	○	○

18.   15 − 6 = ☐

7	8	10	11	NH
○	○	○	○	○

STOP

73

Unit 7: Listening

LISTENING FOR WORD MEANINGS

Directions: Darken the circle beside the word or words that best complete the sentence you hear.

Try This	Listen for key words in each sentence. Then read each answer choice to yourself. Decide which answer choice matches the key words and makes the most sense in the sentence.

Sample A

- ○ pair of shorts
- ○ smile
- ○ new haircut

Think It Through	The correct answer is smile. To grin means the same thing as to smile.

STOP

1. ○ dripping
   ○ screaming
   ○ breaking

2. ○ walked
   ○ ran away
   ○ wandered

3. ○ summer
   ○ fall
   ○ winter

4. ○ move forward
   ○ move backward
   ○ move beyond

5. ○ forest
   ○ beach
   ○ library

6. ○ without warning
   ○ after a long time
   ○ in a mad way

7. ○ think something will happen
   ○ look at something very well
   ○ give a reward

8. ○ silly
   ○ gloomy
   ○ clever

STOP

Name _____   Date _____

CHOOSING PICTURE ANSWERS

Directions: Darken the circle for the correct answer.

Try This	Listen very carefully. Look at the pictures given in each row. Then find the picture that answers the question about the story.

Sample A

○   ○   ○

Think It Through	You should have darkened the circle for the <u>third</u> picture. Mei's mother gave her old clothes to play <u>dress-up</u> with.

🛑 STOP

1.

○   ○   ○

2.

○   ○   ○

3.

○   ○   ○

4.

○   ○   ○

🛑 STOP

Unit 7
Core Skills Test Prep, Grade 2

BUILDING LISTENING SKILLS

Directions: Darken the circle for the correct answer.

Try This	Listen very carefully to the story. As each answer choice is read, think about the answer that makes the most sense.

Sample A

- ○ mows the lawn
- ○ goes grocery shopping
- ○ sweeps the porch

Think It Through	You should have darkened the circle for the second answer choice, goes grocery shopping. The story said that Joseph goes grocery shopping first.

STOP

1. ○ a kite
   ○ a yoyo
   ○ a ball

2. ○ cookies
   ○ candy
   ○ cake

3. ○ disturb the animals
   ○ be asked to leave
   ○ have to pay extra

4. ○ shout
   ○ talk
   ○ pet the animals

5. ○ a talent show
   ○ a magic show
   ○ a puppet show

6. ○ "An Earth Day Celebration"
   ○ "How to Save Water"
   ○ "A Fall Festival"

7. ○ "View of the Grand Canyon"
   ○ "Visiting a President's Ranch"
   ○ "Seeing a Cattle Ranch"
   ○ "A Texas Tour"

8. ○ the beach
   ○ the Alamo
   ○ the state capital
   ○ Yellowstone National Park

STOP

76

TEST

Sample A
- ○ extra
- ○ whole
- ○ special

STOP

1. ○ last
   ○ first
   ○ next

2. ○ take part
   ○ keep score
   ○ watch

3. ○ an answer
   ○ a report
   ○ a picture

4. ○ go out
   ○ flicker
   ○ blaze

5. ○ set down
   ○ throw
   ○ put away

6. ○ happy
   ○ allowed
   ○ sure

7. ○ wash
   ○ stack
   ○ eat

8. ○ appreciate
   ○ spend
   ○ save

9. ○ blow
   ○ shake
   ○ shine

10. ○ sunset
    ○ sunrise
    ○ noon

11. ○ sad
    ○ rough
    ○ playful

12. ○ rain
    ○ soil
    ○ sun

13. ○ sad
    ○ happy
    ○ angry

GO ON

Name _____   Date _____

Sample B

◯   ◯   ◯

──────────────────────────────── 🛑

14.

◯   ◯   ◯

────────────────────────────────

15.

◯   ◯   ◯

────────────────────────────────

16.

◯   ◯   ◯

────────────────────────────────

17.

◯   ◯   ◯

18.

◯   ◯   ◯

────────────────────────────────

19.

◯   ◯   ◯

────────────────────────────────

20.

◯   ◯   ◯

────────────────────────────────

21.

◯   ◯   ◯

🛑

Unit 7
Core Skills Test Prep, Grade 2

Sample C
- ○ a bird
- ○ an airplane
- ○ a rocket

22.
- ○ fall out of the nest
- ○ get stolen by someone
- ○ hatch into baby birds

23.
- ○ swimming in a river
- ○ flipping around in the fishbowl
- ○ swimming off the cardboard
- ○ jumping into the fishbowl

24.
- ○ a bank
- ○ a school
- ○ a river
- ○ a store

25.
- ○ park
- ○ shopping mall
- ○ school
- ○ library

26.
- ○ "The Balloon"
- ○ "Ocean Creatures"
- ○ "A Strange Kind of Fish"
- ○ "Pretty Pets"

27.
- ○ in a pond
- ○ in large lakes
- ○ near coral reefs

28.
- ○ happy
- ○ sad
- ○ afraid

29.
- ○ "A Summer Day"
- ○ "Taking Care of Pets"
- ○ "Carlos Bathes the Dog"

30.
- ○ rinse the soap off
- ○ hook up the water hose
- ○ make lots of suds

31.
- ○ a ruler
- ○ a pencil
- ○ some stickers
- ○ a crayon

32.
- ○ at an airport
- ○ at a bus station
- ○ at home

79

Unit 8: Language

LISTENING TO STORIES

Directions: Darken the circle for the correct answer.

Try This	Listen very carefully. Look at the pictures given in each row. Then find the picture that answers the question about the passage.

Sample A

   ○   ○   ○

Think It Through	You should have darkened the circle for the <u>first</u> picture. In the poem, <u>dress</u> rhymes with <u>mess</u>.

STOP

I.

   ○   ○   ○

2.

   ○   ○   ○

3.

   ○   ○   ○

GO ON

Sample B

- ○ a math book
- ○ a cookbook
- ○ a reading book

STOP

4.

- ○ dragon
- ○ witch
- ○ princess

5.

- ○ "The Princess and the Witch"
- ○ "The Class Play"
- ○ "Our Teacher, Mr. Harris"

6.

- ○ a fish
- ○ a dog
- ○ a snake

7.

- ○ makes her bed
- ○ washes the dishes
- ○ does her homework

STOP

PREWRITING, COMPOSING, AND EDITING

Directions: Darken the circle for the correct answer, or write the answer on the blank lines.

Try This	Listen carefully to the story. Look at the answer choices for the story. Then find the one that best answers the question.

Sample A

A Letter from Camp

Letter to My Family

The food at school is good.	I like to sail in the morning.	We have fun swimming when it is hot.
○	○	○

Think It Through	You should have darkened the circle for the <u>first</u> choice. The answer is *The food at school is good.* Max wanted to write about camp activities in his letter.

 STOP

GO ON

Soccer Fun

Soccer is my favorite sport.
I like to run up and down the field.
Sometimes the ball I take away from the other team.
It is fun when I score a goal.

1. ○ I play soccer after school.
   ○ My mother watches me play soccer.
   ○ Everyone cheers for me.

2. ○ The ball I take away sometimes from the other team.
   ○ Sometimes I take the ball away from the other team.
   ○ Correct the way it is.

A Kick Out of Soccer

3. ○ watch a soccer game
   ○ draw a picture of herself playing soccer
   ○ make a list of reasons she likes soccer

4. _____

   _____

   _____

GO ON

The name of my team is the Panthers.

We practice two times each week.

To warm up, we <u>running</u> around the field.
               (I)

We also <u>kick</u> the ball to each other.
              (2)

My best friends are on my team.

We have so much fun together.

5.   kicking   kicked   Correct the way it is.
            ○   ○   ○

6.   ran   run   Correct the way it is.
            ○   ○   ○

My Trip

7.

van ○   train ○   water ○

8.

A Book About My Trip

| Places we camped ○ | Places we visited ○ | Places we wanted to visit ○ |

Table of Contents

9.   rocks ○   oceans ○   cactus ○

STOP

Unit 8
Core Skills Test Prep, Grade 2

We saw a very tall cactus in the desert.
We asked a park ranger about it.
The park ranger's name was <u>Mr. elkhorn</u>.
                                    (1)

He said, "<u>A flower</u> will bloom on the cactus after it rains."
          (2)

10.

_____

_____

_____

11.   A Flower   a flower   Correct the way it is.
           ○   ○   ○

Travel Fun

My family went on a trip in June.
We slept in a tent every night.
My father cooked over a campfire.
We sang songs in school.
We went to many interesting places.

12. ○ My family went on a trip in June.

○ My father cooked over a campfire.

○ We sang songs in school.

13. ○ We had a picnic in the park.

○ The huge waves crashed against the white sand.

○ I bought some colorful postcards.

FINDING MISSPELLED WORDS

Directions: Darken the circle for the underlined word that is <u>not</u> spelled correctly.

Try This	Look at each of the underlined words carefully and say each of these words silently to yourself. Decide which words you know are spelled correctly. Then look at the other words to make your choice.

Sample A

The <u>magical</u> king <u>granted</u> the shoemaker three <u>wishs</u>.
    ○   ○   ○

Think It Through	You should have darkened the circle for the last underlined word. <u>Wishs</u> is the word that is not spelled correctly. <u>Wishes</u> is spelled w-i-s-h-e-s.

I. The car <u>started</u> <u>slideing</u> on the icy <u>highway</u>.
   ○   ○   ○

2. The <u>wave</u> <u>carryed</u> the shell onto the <u>beach</u>.
   ○   ○   ○

3. <u>Please</u> <u>sit</u> on the <u>char</u>.
   ○   ○   ○

4. Carley <u>loves</u> to <u>read</u> <u>storys</u> about pirates.
   ○   ○   ○

5. The <u>puppy</u> was sitting up and <u>beging</u> for a <u>treat</u>.
   ○   ○   ○

STOP

TEST

Sample A

 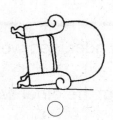 

○ ○ ○

 STOP

1.

○ ○ ○

2.

○ ○ ○

3.

○ ○ ○

4.

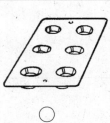  

○ ○ ○

GO ON

Sample B

○ "Mel Plays with a Baby"

○ "Bedtime for Baby"

○ "Mel's Baby-sitting Job"

STOP

5.

○ fed the baby a bottle

○ rocked the baby to sleep

○ gave the baby a bath

6.

_____

_____

7.

○ a frog

○ a rabbit

○ a donkey

8.

○ lose the clock

○ forget to set the clock

○ break the clock

GO ON

Name _____ Date _____

Sample C

About Heather's Father

Writing a Story		
Talk to her father ○	Visit the newspaper office ○	Read a book about her town ○

9. ○ Ride in a police car

   ○ Watch a movie about police officers

   ○ Make a list of questions to ask her father

A Police Officer's Job

My father is a police officer.
He has an important job.
My bike has a flat tire.
He helps people who are hurt.
Sometimes he directs cars.

10. _____

    _____

    _____

▶ GO ON

Unit 8
Core Skills Test Prep, Grade 2

Going to the Moon

Table of Contents

11. ○ The big holes on the moon

○ The miles between the earth and moon

○ The first person who visited the moon

12. _____

_____

GO ON

The big holes <u>is</u> called craters.
(1)
I would <u>like</u> to go inside a crater.
(2)
It would be like walking inside a cave.

13. _____

_____

14. ○ liking

○ likes

○ Correct the way it is.

Seeing the Moon

The moon is very far away.
I would like to ride in a spaceship to get there.
A spacesuit I could wear to keep me safe.
I would like to see what is in the moon's big holes.

15. ○ When I get older, I want to visit the moon.

○ The big holes are deep.

○ A spaceship moves very fast.

16. ○ A spacesuit to keep me safe I could wear.

○ I could wear a spacesuit to keep me safe.

○ Correct the way it is.

►GO ON►

Visiting Aunt Donna

Dear Aunt Donna,

Thank you for inviting me to visit.
The farm this summer.
<u>May I stay for two weeks</u>
I want to learn how to take care of animals.

17. _____

_____

_____

18. ○ I want to milk and feed the cows and chickens.

○ The cows I want to milk and the chickens I want to feed.

○ I want to milk the cows and feed the chickens.

19.   weeks?   weeks.   weeks!

      ○   ○   ○

GO ON

> I am leaving this <u>tuesday</u>.
>   **(I)**
> <u>Will you pick me up at the bus station</u>
> **(2)**
> I can't wait to see you.
> Love,
> Shakia

20. _____

_____

_____

21.   Tues Day   Tuesday   Correct the way it is.
             ○   ○   ○

GO ON

Sample D

My <u>sister</u> is <u>arriveing</u> <u>tomorrow</u> from Canada.
    ◯   ◯   ◯

🛑 STOP

_____

22. <u>Wher</u> <u>does</u> your <u>family</u> like to swim?
   ◯   ◯   ◯

_____

23. Go <u>down</u> the hall and <u>tern</u> to the <u>right</u>.
     ◯   ◯   ◯

_____

24. The <u>frog</u> was <u>hoping</u> along the <u>path</u>.
     ◯   ◯   ◯

_____

25. <u>Your</u> <u>dog</u> is very <u>frendly</u>.
   ◯   ◯   ◯

_____

26. <u>Watr</u> the plants <u>before</u> you <u>leave</u>.
   ◯   ◯   ◯

_____

27. We saw many <u>interesting</u> <u>butterflys</u> in the <u>woods</u>.
      ◯   ◯   ◯

_____

28. Grandpa gave me <u>three</u> big <u>pushs</u> on the <u>swing</u>.
      ◯   ◯   ◯

_____

29. The <u>boxs</u> were <u>stacked</u> in the <u>corner</u>.
   ◯   ◯   ◯

🛑 STOP

_____

Unit 9: Practice Test 1

 You have 35 minutes to complete this test.

READING COMPREHENSION

Sample A

Going to School

Jim lives on a farm. The farm is five miles from his school. He rides a bus to school because he lives too far to walk.

How does Jim get to school?
- ○ He walks.
- ○ His mom drives him in a car.
- ○ He rides a horse.
- ○ He rides a bus.

Curtis's Jobs

Mr. Ford asked Curtis to do some jobs. Curtis likes to help Mr. Ford. Mr. Ford always gives him a dollar for each job.

Curtis got a hose and soap. He washed the windows, the doors, and the trunk. Finally, Curtis washed the tires.

When Curtis was done, Mr. Ford looked at the car. "You worked very hard. I will give you two dollars," said Mr. Ford. "Tomorrow morning you will need a rake. I will pay you two more dollars if you do as well."

"Thank you, Mr. Ford. I will be back tomorrow," said Curtis.

1. Why did Mr. Ford give Curtis two dollars?
   - ○ Curtis did a good job.
   - ○ Curtis wanted to buy candy.
   - ○ Curtis did two jobs.
   - ○ Curtis needed a loan.

2. What did Curtis wash?
   - ○ a bike
   - ○ a car
   - ○ a house
   - ○ a dog

3. Curtis will go to Mr. Ford's —
   - ○ in the middle of the night.
   - ○ in the morning.
   - ○ in the afternoon.
   - ○ in the evening.

4. You can tell that tomorrow Curtis will —
   - ○ trim trees.
   - ○ mow the grass.
   - ○ sweep the sidewalk.
   - ○ rake leaves.

GO ON

Tia's Ride

Tia lived in the mountains with her family and a donkey named Clyde. Tia and Clyde went everywhere together. Clyde was a good mountain climber. He never slipped or fell. Tia was not as good at climbing. She had to be careful where she walked. When the path was dangerous, Tia would ride on Clyde's back. Tia rode the donkey on the path down to the stream. There were fish swimming in the stream. Tia and the donkey splashed in the cool, clear water. Later when they returned home, Tia gave Clyde a pail of food. Then Tia went inside for dinner.

5. The boxes show things that happened in the story.

Tia rode the donkey down to the stream.		Tia gave Clyde a pail of food.
I	2	3

What belongs in Box 2?

○ Tia went inside the house for dinner.

○ Clyde slipped on the path to the stream.

○ Tia and Clyde caught some fish.

○ Tia and Clyde splashed in the water.

6. What is another good name for this story?

○ "Walking in the Mountains"

○ "A Girl and Her Donkey"

○ "How to Train a Donkey"

○ "Fishing in Mountain Streams"

7. Where did Tia and Clyde live?

○ on a farm

○ in the mountains

○ in the city

○ by a store

8. Why did Tia ride the donkey to the stream?

○ The donkey was tired.

○ The path was long.

○ The path was dangerous.

○ The donkey hurt his foot.

▶GO ON◀

Telling a Tree's Age

Have you ever looked closely at the top of a tree stump? You might see many rings. The rings are often narrow near the center of the tree and wider near the outside.

Each ring stands for a year of growth. As a tree grows, more and more rings are added. After the tree has been cut down, you can see the rings on the stump. The number of rings tells the tree's age. The more rings you count, the older the tree is.

9. Each ring stands for —

○ 1 inch of growth.

○ the height of the tree.

○ when the tree was cut.

○ a year of growth.

10. How do you find the age of a tree?

○ see if the rings are wide or narrow

○ count the leaves

○ count the rings

○ see how tall it is

11. What can you say about a tree with few rings?

○ It is old.

○ It is young.

○ It is tall.

○ It needs water.

12. What is the best way to find out more about trees?

○ recycle paper

○ plant a garden

○ read a book about the life of a tree

○ read a list of things made from wood

▶GO ON

Peanut Butter and Banana Bun

You will need:

I hot dog bun

I tablespoon peanut butter

I banana

Follow these steps:

1. Spread the peanut butter on the bun.
2. Peel the banana and set it in the bun.
3. Slice the bun in half and serve one half per person.

If you like, you can add an *optional* topping. Sprinkle on coconut or pour on a little bit of honey. Or, think of your own special topping. "Peanut Butter and Banana Bun" is great with or without toppings.

13. Right after you spread the peanut butter, you should —

○ slice the bun in half.

○ serve the bun.

○ spread butter.

○ add the banana.

14. "Peanut Butter and Banana Bun" is most like a —

○ soup.

○ sandwich.

○ salad.

○ cookie.

15. How many servings will each banana and bun make?

○ four

○ three

○ two

○ one

16. In these directions, *optional* means —

○ something you may or may not do.

○ something you must do.

○ something you cook.

○ something you taste.

▶ GO ON ▶

Unit 9
Core Skills Test Prep, Grade 2

Maciel Visits the Lighthouse

Maciel and her mother went to the beach in Cape May, New Jersey, last summer. One day they went to see the lighthouse.

Maciel and her mom climbed to the top of the tower. From there they could see very far. They saw miles of ocean and beach. It was a beautiful sight.

Mr. Foreman, the man who works at the lighthouse, told Maciel and her mom all about it. The Cape May Lighthouse is over 130 years old. It is all white, and it is 165 feet tall. It has a very strong light. Mr. Foreman said that the lighthouse is still very important to sailors. Sailors can see its light from 24 miles out at sea. The light helps ships come into Delaware Bay.

Mr. Foreman told Maciel and her mom how the sailors take care of the lighthouse. Their *tasks* are cleaning the light and making sure it is working. Mr. Foreman said that many people who live in Cape May also help keep the lighthouse in good shape. They want others to enjoy it for many years to come. Some people help fix parts of the lighthouse. Some clean the lighthouse. Others paint it.

Maciel can't wait to visit the lighthouse again next summer. She wants Mr. Foreman to show the lighthouse to her best friend, Josephine.

GO ON

17. In this story, Mr. Foreman is —

○ a sailor who cleans the light at the lighthouse.

○ the man who works at the lighthouse.

○ Maciel's father.

○ Maciel's best friend.

18. Why is it important to take care of the lighthouse?

○ so that Mr. Foreman can have a job

○ so people can look out of the tower

○ so that sailors at sea can find land

○ so that visitors have a place to go

19. How does Maciel feel at the end of the story?

○ She is tired and wants to leave.

○ She wants to live in the lighthouse.

○ She worries that sailors do not take care of the lighthouse.

○ She is excited about the visit and wants to come back.

20. What does the word *tasks* in this story mean?

○ jobs

○ friends

○ joys

○ games

21. This story was written mainly to —

○ tell about big ships.

○ ask for help in fixing the lighthouse.

○ tell about a special lighthouse.

○ tell how to build a lighthouse.

22. Which of these is another good name for this story?

○ "Maciel and Her Mom Have Fun at the Beach"

○ "A Visit to a Lighthouse"

○ "Sailing in Delaware Bay"

○ "How to Take Care of a Lighthouse"

GO ON

All About Ducks

Ducks are interesting birds. They can fly in the air, and they can walk on the land. Mostly, they like to swim in the water. Ponds and streams are full of good things to eat. There are little fish, big bugs, and tender plants. Ducks can swim very fast. They have big feet for pushing the water. They cannot walk as fast as they swim. On land, ducks must be careful. A fox or a wolf might catch them.

23. What is another good name for this passage?

○ "Why Ducks Like Water"

○ "Why Ducks Fly"

○ "What Ducks Like to Eat"

○ "How to Catch a Duck"

24. How do big feet help ducks?

○ Big feet help them walk fast.

○ Big feet help them catch bugs.

○ Big feet help them push the water.

○ Big feet help them hide from foxes.

25. What is something that ducks do not do?

○ swim

○ climb

○ walk

○ fly

26. Why might a fox want to catch a duck?

○ to eat it

○ to play with it

○ to see who is faster

○ to learn to swim

STOP

Unit 10: Practice Test 2

 You have 20 minutes to complete this test.

READING VOCABULARY, PART 1

Sample A

neighbor ○   money ○   starfish ○

STOP

1. sorry ○   circus ○   ladybug ○

2. open ○   inside ○   under ○

3. before ○   something ○   story ○

4. balloon ○   myself ○   making ○

5. quiet ○   again ○   cupcake ○

6. penny ○   wishing ○   suitcase ○

Sample B

quicker ○   quickest ○   quickly ○

STOP

7. working ○   worker ○   worked ○

8. runner ○   runs ○   running ○

9. fills ○   filling ○   filled ○

10. adds ○   adding ○   added ○

11. rains ○   rained ○   raining ○

12. softest ○   softer ○   softly ○

STOP

103

Sample C

who'd ○	who'll ○	who's ○

_____ STOP

13.
it'll ○	it's ○	it'd ○

14.
I'm ○	I've ○	I'd ○

15.
don't ○	doesn't ○	didn't ○

16.
isn't ○	aren't ○	weren't ○

17.
can't ○	couldn't ○	weren't ○

18.
could've ○	couldn't ○	can't ○

Sample D

sp<u>a</u>ce

cap ○	center ○	chase ○

_____ 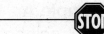 STOP

19. <u>n</u>ear
rocky ○	speed ○	knee ○

20. <u>t</u>ime
shy ○	lip ○	feel ○

21. st<u>r</u>ong
toe ○	mouth ○	jaw ○

22. <u>b</u>ow
front ○	road ○	should ○

23. v<u>oi</u>ce
lost ○	enjoy ○	who ○

24. <u>h</u>opped
locking ○	only ○	worn ○

 STOP

READING VOCABULARY, PART 2

Sample A

Something that is tiny is —
- ○ metal.
- ○ broken.
- ○ small.
- ○ rich.

STOP

1. Closer means —
- ○ nearer.
- ○ around.
- ○ away.
- ○ farther.

2. To whisper is to —
- ○ talk softly.
- ○ play a game.
- ○ run a race.
- ○ sing loudly.

3. To hunt means to —
- ○ talk.
- ○ sit on.
- ○ break.
- ○ look for.

4. If something is still, it is not —
- ○ sorry.
- ○ strong.
- ○ moving.
- ○ sleeping.

5. A carpet is most like a —
- ○ chair.
- ○ window.
- ○ rug.
- ○ truck.

6. Foolish means —
- ○ next.
- ○ silly.
- ○ last.
- ○ sleepy.

7. A subway is a kind of —
- ○ train.
- ○ walk.
- ○ book.
- ○ number.

8. A chuckle is a kind of —
- ○ song.
- ○ laugh.
- ○ story.
- ○ river.

9. A dish is most like a —
- ○ desk.
- ○ plate.
- ○ pillow.
- ○ cup.

STOP

Sample B

> We ate lunch out on the deck.

In which sentence does deck mean the same as it does above?

○ Let's deck the room with streamers.

○ I'll get a deck of cards.

○ Jake built a new wood deck.

○ I'm on the top deck of the boat.

10.

> Is it my turn to bat?

In which sentence does bat mean the same as it does above?

○ A bat is an interesting animal.

○ Please hand me the other bat.

○ Let's bat some ideas around.

○ I will bat the ball to the fence.

11.

> Can you float on your back in the water?

In which sentence does float mean the same as it does above?

○ Dad made me a root beer float.

○ Which float did you like?

○ The small boat began to float on the lake.

○ Carol had a float to play with in the pool.

12.

> We watched the sun dip below the trees.

Write a sentence in which dip means the same as it does above.

_____

_____

_____

_____

13.

> We climbed over the steep bank to the lake.

In which sentence does bank mean the same as it does above?

○ My bank is in a big, gray building.

○ She has a new purple piggy bank.

○ Don't bank on his promise.

○ Flowers grow along the river bank.

Sample C

Uncle Luis <u>repaired</u> the broken machine. <u>Repaired</u> means —

- ○ fixed.
- ○ sold.
- ○ lost.
- ○ washed.

STOP

14. That painting is <u>famous</u> all over the world. <u>Famous</u> means —

- ○ well-known.
- ○ cheap.
- ○ new.
- ○ funny.

15. The bridge is closely <u>modeled</u> after one in England. <u>Modeled</u> means —

- ○ paid.
- ○ painted.
- ○ added.
- ○ copied.

16. I tried but I couldn't <u>budge</u> the heavy box. <u>Budge</u> means —

- ○ buy.
- ○ pack.
- ○ move.
- ○ seal.

17. It is dangerous to play with matches because they could <u>harm</u> someone. <u>Harm</u> means —

- ○ look.
- ○ hurt.
- ○ help.
- ○ hear.

18. He will <u>compose</u> a new song for the movie. What does <u>compose</u> mean?

_____

_____

19. Her truck has <u>tough</u> tires that last a long time. <u>Tough</u> means —

- ○ little.
- ○ strong.
- ○ many.
- ○ old.

20. We tried to be quiet and <u>conceal</u> the surprise. <u>Conceal</u> means —

- ○ hide.
- ○ miss.
- ○ show.
- ○ end.

STOP

Unit 11: Practice Test 3

You have 50 minutes to complete this test.

MATH PROBLEM SOLVING

Sample A

300 + 10   3,010 ○   310 ○   30,010 ○   3,100 ○

STOP

1.

○   ○   ○   ○

2.

234 ○   2,034 ○   20,304 ○   200,304 ○

3.

43		68

39 ○   41 ○   55 ○   71 ○

4.

173 ○   1,730 ○   1,073 ○   10,073 ○

5.

_____

_____

 GO ON

Unit 11
Core Skills Test Prep, Grade 2

6.

4×3

$4 + 3$	$3 + 3 + 3 + 3$	$4 - 3$	$4 + 4 + 4$
◯	◯	◯	◯

7.

$\boxed{821}$

_____

_____

8.

◯   ◯   ◯   ◯

9.

$4 + \square = 4$

0	1	4	8
◯	◯	◯	◯

10.

◯ $10 + 9 = 19$ ◯ $10 - 8 = 2$

◯ $9 - 1 = 8$ ◯ $9 + 1 = 10$

Unit 11
Core Skills Test Prep, Grade 2

11.

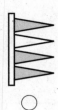 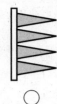 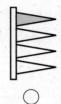 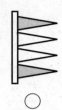

   ○   ○   ○   ○

12.

36	33		27	24

25   30   34   35
○   ○   ○   ○

13.

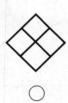   

   ○   ○   ○   ○

14.

73 74 75   ○   ○   ○   ○

15.

 | $\frac{1}{4}$ $\frac{1}{5}$ $\frac{4}{5}$ $\frac{4}{1}$
                                   ○   ○   ○   ○

GO ON

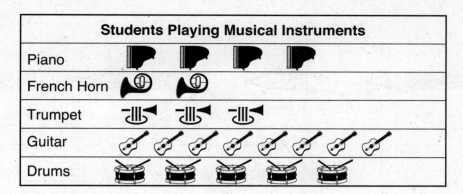

Students Playing Musical Instruments

Piano	
French Horn	
Trumpet	
Guitar	
Drums	

Each instrument = 1 student

16.

4	5	8	9
○	○	○	○

17. _____

_____

18.

	▷		▭
○	○	○	○

19.

Lou	Laurie	Alex	Patti
ㅐㅐ ㅐㅐ	ㅐㅐ	/	///

_____

_____

GO ON

Unit 11
Core Skills Test Prep, Grade 2

20.

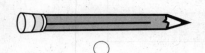  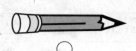 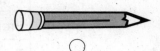

○   ○   ○   ○

21.

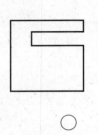 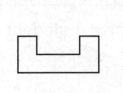 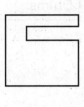

○   ○   ○   ○

22.

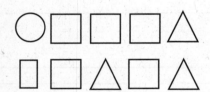

○   ○   ○   ○

23.

2:15   3:15   2:45   3:45
○   ○   ○   ○

24.

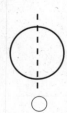 

○   ○   ○   ○

GO ON →

25.

      5   7   8   9

      ◯   ◯   ◯   ◯

26.

                             6¢   11¢   26¢   30¢

                             ◯   ◯   ◯   ◯

27.

28.

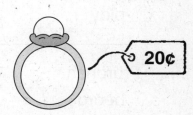

     4¢   12¢   15¢   17¢

      ◯   ◯   ◯   ◯

29.

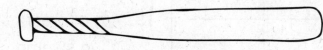

      6   7   9   12

      ◯   ◯   ◯   ◯

STOP

Unit 11

Core Skills Test Prep, Grade 2

Unit 12: Practice Test 4

 You have 25 minutes to complete this test.

LISTENING

Sample A
- ○ talk about
- ○ think about
- ○ look for

STOP

1. ○ growl   ○ jump   ○ bite

2. ○ four weeks
   ○ several hours
   ○ seven days

3. ○ run
   ○ walk
   ○ play

4. ○ branch
   ○ board
   ○ ladder

5. ○ writer
   ○ dancer
   ○ baker

6. ○ an answer
   ○ a visitor
   ○ a new dish

7. ○ say hello
   ○ tell a story
   ○ give a signal

8. ○ droop   ○ grow   ○ open

9. ○ purse
   ○ suitcase
   ○ billfold

10. ○ country
    ○ city
    ○ state

11. ○ slow
    ○ quick
    ○ careful

12. ○ even
    ○ bigger
    ○ angry

13. ○ a forest
    ○ a swamp
    ○ a jungle

STOP

Unit 12
Core Skills Test Prep, Grade 2

Name _____   Date _____

Sample B

○   ○   ○

STOP

18.

          ○

14.

19.

     ○

15.

20.

○   ○   ○

16.

     ○

21.

17.

          ○

STOP

Sample C

- ○ a ball
- ○ a stump
- ○ a friend

STOP

22.
- ○ children over ten
- ○ dogs
- ○ plastic containers

23.
- ○ carry it home
- ○ bury it in the sand
- ○ put it in the trash containers

24.
- ○ make a salad
- ○ set the table
- ○ make lemonade

25.
- ○ mother
- ○ father
- ○ grandmother

26.
- ○ nest
- ○ bird
- ○ statue
- ○ birdbath

27.
- ○ large sticks
- ○ grass
- ○ leaves
- ○ small rocks

28.
- ○ only one year
- ○ two years
- ○ three years
- ○ many years

29.
- ○ boring place
- ○ scary place
- ○ lonely place
- ○ wonderful place

30.
- ○ magazines
- ○ videos
- ○ baseball cards
- ○ different kinds of books

31.
- ○ paying money
- ○ doing work
- ○ making a promise
- ○ mailing in a coupon

STOP

Unit 13: Practice Test 5

LANGUAGE

You have 35 minutes to complete this test.

Sample A

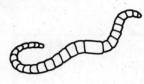

○　　　　　　○　　　　　　○

STOP

1.

○　　　　　　○　　　　　　○

2.

○　　　　　　○　　　　　　○

3.

○　　　　　　○　　　　　　○

4.

○　　　　　　○　　　　　　○

GO ON

Unit 13
Core Skills Test Prep, Grade 2

Name _____ Date _____

Sample B

- ○ made a salad
- ○ set the table
- ○ made a pitcher of lemonade

STOP

5. ○ a fish
   ○ a heron
   ○ a boy

6. ○ "Janey's Job"
   ○ "A Mother's Day Surprise"
   ○ "Washing Clothes"

7. _____

   _____

8. ○ a bugle
   ○ a drum
   ○ a bell

GO ON

Sample C

> I <u>hope</u> to see you at my party.
> Please let me know if you can come.
>   Your friend,
>   Ingrid

hoped   hoping   Correct the way it is.
○   ○   ○

Sample D

> I am having a birthday party.
> On Friday at two o'clock.
> We will play games at my house.

○ I am having a birthday party.

○ On Friday at two o'clock.

○ We will play games at my house.

Sample E

My Birthday Party

Writing Invitations

| The people she will invite | The time of the party | Where the party will be |

○   ○   ○

A Big Breakfast

I was hungry when I woke up.

I poured a glass of milk for everyone.

A glass of orange juice I also drank.

Father made banana muffins.

---

9. _____

_____

_____

10. ○ I also drank a glass of orange juice.

○ I drank a glass also of orange juice.

○ Correct the way it is.

Healthy Food

11. ○ ask his mother what his family will eat for dinner

○ make a list of healthy foods

○ think about the food he ate during the day

---

12. ○ to find out if he eats good food

○ to write a food menu

○ to tell about his favorite foods

▶ **GO ON**

I <u>gone</u> to a friend's house for dinner.
  (I)

We ate hot dogs.

Hot dogs <u>are</u> my favorite food.
       (2)

We had salad and peas, too.

Of course, I drank another glass of milk.

13.   is   was   Correct the way it is.
          ◯   ◯   ◯

14. _____

_____

© Houghton Mifflin Harcourt Publishing Company

Talking to Grandmother

15.
         hay   chicken   train
         ○   ○   ○

16.

In Grandma's Time		
How people traveled	Games people played	Where Grandma lives
○	○	○

Table of Contents

17.
    long skirts   milking cows   riding horses
     ○   ○   ○

GO ON

Unit 13

Core Skills Test Prep, Grade 2

When Grandma was Young

Grandma lived on a farm when she was little.

The family grew most of their own food.

They grew corn, beans, and potatoes.

Grandma shops at the store on Friday.

They had to raise cows and chickens for meat.

18. ○ Grandma cooked food in a big black pan on a wood stove.

○ The stove made the kitchen hot in the summer.

○ Grandma helped make bread every day.

_____

19. _____

_____

The family could not grow everything they needed.

They had to buy things like flour and sugar.

"Are you ready for some fun?" Great Grandpa would ask.
(1)

Then the family knew it was time to go to town.

They would visit mr barton's store.
                              (2)

20.   mr. Barton's   Mr. Barton's   Correct the way it is.
                     ○   ○   ○

_____

21.   are you ready   Are you Ready   Correct the way it is.
                     ○   ○   ○

▶ GO ON ◀

Core Skills Test Prep, Grade 2

Going Fishing

22.
Table of contents   Title page   First chapter
○   ○   ○

A Rainbow Fish

I went fishing.

On Saturday morning.

I caught a fish I have never seen before.

23. ○ Pink and blue stripes the fish had on its body.

○ On its body pink and blue stripes the fish had.

○ The fish had pink and blue stripes on its body.

24. ○ I went fishing.

○ On Saturday morning.

○ I caught a fish I have never seen before.

▶GO ON

I did not know what kind of fish it was.

I went to the library to look in a book.

"Where are the books about fish" I asked.
(1)

The librarian helped me.

I found a picture of the fish.
      (2)

It was called a rainbow trout.

25.   finding   finds   Correct the way it is.
           ○   ○   ○

26. _____

_____

Name _____   Date _____

STOP

Sample F

Flashs of light appeared during the storm.
○   ○   ○

27. Dad bought two new leashs for our dog.
        ○   ○   ○

28. Grover is diging a hole to bury his dog bone.
                    ○   ○   ○

29. Angie is bakeing a birthday cake.
                ○   ○   ○

30. John walkt to the store to buy milk.
            ○   ○   ○

GO ON

31. The <u>baby</u> <u>cryed</u> herself to <u>sleep</u>.
     ◯   ◯   ◯

_____

32. Water is <u>driping</u> off the <u>roof</u> of the <u>house</u>.
         ◯   ◯   ◯

_____

33. Do you <u>like</u> to eat <u>cherrys</u> for a <u>snack</u>?
       ◯   ◯   ◯

_____

34. We are <u>moveing</u> to <u>another</u> <u>state</u>.
       ◯   ◯   ◯

STOP

INDIVIDUAL RECORD FORM

	Pages	Number of Questions	Number Right
Reading Comprehension			
Reading Selections	33–38	22	
Test	39–42	17	
Reading Vocabulary			
Understanding Word Meanings	43	6	
Matching Words with More Than One Meaning	44	2	
Using Context Clues	45	4	
Recognizing Compound Words	46	8	
Choosing Correct Words	47	8	
Recognizing Contractions	48	8	
Matching Word Sounds	49	8	
Test	50–53	24	
Math Problem Solving and Procedures			
Understanding Numeration	57	3	
Using Whole Numbers, Fractions, and Decimals	58	4	
Working with Patterns and Relationships	59	3	
Working with Statistics and Probability	60	2	
Working with Geometry	61	3	
Working with Measurement	62	3	
Solving Problems	63	4	
Understanding Computation	64–65	14	
Using Computation	66	6	
Test 1: Math Procedures	67–68	18	
Test 2: Math Problem Solving	69–73	26	
Listening			
Listening for Word Meanings	74	8	
Choosing Picture Answers	75	4	
Building Listening Skills	76	8	
Test	77–79	32	
Language			
Listening to Stories	80–81	7	
Prewriting, Composing, and Editing	82–86	13	
Finding Misspelled Words	87	5	
Test	88–95	29	
Practice Test 1			
Reading Comprehension	96–102	26	
Practice Test 2			
Reading Vocabulary, Part 1	103–104	24	
Reading Vocabulary, Part 2	105–107	20	
Practice Test 3			
Math Problem Solving	108–113	29	
Practice Test 4			
Listening	114–116	31	
Practice Test 5			
Language	117–127	34	

Individual Record Form
Core Skills Test Prep, Grade 2

Scripts and Answers

- Every skill lesson, Unit Test, and Practice Test begins with sample questions.
- Please do the sample questions together with your child. Go over any questions your child may have.
- For the skill lessons, read the directions and go over the **Try This** strategy before beginning the sample question. After your child has answered the question, go over the answer using the **Think It Through** feature.

- As you read the scripts, allow plenty of time for your child to answer the question before moving on to the next item.
- In the following scripts, the sections that begin with the word **Say** are to be read out loud to your child. The answers for each page are located immediately following the scripts.

Unit 2

Pages 7–12

Say: Look at the first passage. Read the passage silently. Then answer the question that follows: "In this paragraph, the word *higher* means—" Darken the circle for the correct answer.

Say: The correct answer is the first choice. *Higher* means "more than high." The suffix *-er* means "more than."

Say: Now you will practice answering questions about determining word meanings. Read each passage carefully and answer the questions that follow. Darken the circle for the correct answer.

Answers: Pages 7–8

1. more than high, **2.** the most warm, **3.** how he will run, **4.** the cupcakes were made already, **5.** more than tall, **6.** it is taking place right now

Answers: Pages 9–10

1. not easy, **2.** big, **3.** hurt us, **4.** follow directions, **5.** to hit, **6.** helpful

Answers: Pages 11–12

1. to make wet, **2.** finish, **3.** to make, **4.** smile, **5.** jumped, **6.** stop

Pages 13–20

Say: Look at the first passage. Read the passage silently. Then answer the question that follows: "Faster boats were first built —" Darken the circle for the correct answer.

Say: The correct answer is the first answer choice: "Faster boats were first built 5,000 years ago." The first sentence in the second paragraph says, "Things changed 5,000 years ago."

Say: Now you will practice answering more questions about identifying supporting ideas. Read each passage carefully and answer the questions that follow. Darken the circle for the correct answer.

Answers: Pages 13–14

1. 5,000 years ago, **2.** were hard to make, **3.** they went faster, **4.** fly an airplane, **5.** brothers, **6.** flew on December 17, 1903

Answers: Pages 15–16

1. Babe was sent away to school., **2.** in 1919, **3.** Babe's home run record was broken.

Answers: Pages 17–18

1. sew on buttons for the eyes, **2.** make a list, **3.** Buy the paint and brushes., **4.** Step 5, **5.** clean the brushes

Answers: Pages 19–20

1. New York City, **2.** in 1931, **3.** after the Empire State Building was built, **4.** England, **5.** 1825, **6.** night

Pages 21–24

Say: Look at the first passage. Read the passage silently. Then answer the question that follows: "What is the main idea of this passage?" Darken the circle for the correct answer.

Say: The correct answer is the first choice: "The earth moves around the sun." The first sentence in the paragraph says, "The earth goes around the sun."

Say: Now you will practice answering more questions about summarizing the main idea. Read each passage carefully and answer the questions that follow. Darken the circle for the correct answer.

Answers: Pages 21–22

1. The earth moves around the sun., **2.** Soccer is played by people all over the world., **3.** You will have a good time hiking., **4.** Mother's Day should be a special day., **5.** The winter of 1994 was bad.

Pages 23–24

1. Bats are interesting animals., **2.** Boston is an interesting city to visit., **3.** There are many things to learn about owls., **4.** To bowl, you need some special things., **5.** Jane Addams helped many people.

Pages 25–28

Say: Look at the first passage. Read the passage silently. Then answer the question that follows: "Why couldn't Jill win a race at first?" Darken the circle for the correct answer.

Say: The correct answer is the third choice: "She was not a fast runner." The first sentence in the paragraph says, "Jill could not run very fast."

Say: Now you will practice answering more questions about cause-and-effect relationships and predicting what will happen next. Read each passage carefully and answer the questions that follow. Darken the circle for the correct answer.

Answers: Pages 25–26

1. She was not a fast runner., **2.** She practiced a lot., **3.** Tony watered it., **4.** He cared for the plant and it grew., **5.** She saw he was hurt., **6.** She took good care of him., **7.** She would not have to be alone.

Answers: Pages 27–28

1. He will not have his homework., **2.** go swimming, **3.** Alicia and Herbie will bump into each other., **4.** Chuck and Fatima will have a magic show., **5.** He will go get the ball., **6.** She will take out a book and read.

Pages 29–30

Say: Look at the first passage. Read the passage silently. Then answer the question that follows: "How did Sam feel about the news?" Darken the circle for the correct answer.

Say: The correct answer is the first choice: "He was mad because he did not want to move." Sam says he did not want to go because he wouldn't have any friends.

Say: Now you will practice answering more questions about making inferences and generalizations. Read each passage carefully and answer the questions that follow. Darken the circle for the correct answer.

Answers: Pages 29–30

1. He was mad because he did not want to move., **2.** excited, **3.** Laura was angry., **4.** proud

Pages 31–32

Say: Look at the first passage. Read the passage silently. Then answer the question that follows: "Which of these is a fact from the passage?" Darken the circle for the correct answer.

Say: The correct answer is the second choice: "Most sharks eat plants and fish." Words like *best*, *pretty*, and *should* suggest opinions, not facts.

Say: Now you will practice answering more questions about recognizing the author's point of view and distinguishing between fact and opinion. Read each passage carefully and answer the questions that follow. Darken the circle for the correct answer.

Answers: Pages 31–32

1. Most sharks eat plants and fish., **2.** Maine is a great place to visit., **3.** are in danger, **4.** High jumping can be a lot of fun., **5.** Food is used in many parts of our body.

Unit 3

Pages 33–38

Say: Look at Sample A. Read the story silently. Then answer the question that follows: "What did Mr. Feld's son give him?" Darken the circle for the correct answer.

Say: Look at **Think It Through**. The correct answer is the third choice, "knee pads." The next-to-last sentence says, "Today his son gave him some knee pads."

Say: Now you will practice answering more questions about stories that you read. Do numbers 1 through 22 just as you did Sample A. Read each selection carefully. Darken the circle for the correct answer, or write in your answer.

Answers: Pages 33–38

Sample A: knee pads, **1.** waiting for the bus, **2.** Possible answer: because it was about to rain, **3.** She chewed the net apart., **4.** The lion let the mouse go., **5.** Possible answer: The mouse woke him up., **6.** Little friends can be good friends., **7.** his party, **8.** Possible answer: He misses Harry., **9.** add sugar to water, **10.** a costume party, **11.** friend, **12.** a kind of flavoring, **13.** the day after his party, **14.** where his friend Harry lives, **15.** students who do at least two things from the list, **16.** Possible answer: to help others, **17.** Ms. Salina will speak to them., **18.** your room number, **19.** She was in a school play., **20.** a mouse, **21.** Dawn's part in the school play, **22.** Possible answer: Dawn's Special Part

Test: Pages 39–42

Say: In this test you will use the reading skills that we have practiced in this unit. Look at Sample A. Read the selection silently. Then answer the question that follows: "What should Ellen do first?" Darken the circle for the correct answer.

Say: The correct answer is the first choice, "clean her room." The second sentence in Sample A states that Ellen's mother asked Ellen to clean her room first and then she could read or watch TV.

Unit 4

Page 43

Say: Look at Sample A. Read the sentence and the four answer choices: "To raise something is to — lift it ...count it ...fly it ...open it." Darken the circle beside the word that has the same or almost the same meaning as the underlined word, *raise*.

Say: Look at **Think It Through**. The correct answer is the first choice, "lift it." If you raise something, you lift it up. To raise something is not to count it, fly it, or open it.

Say: Now you will practice matching more words that have the same or almost the same meaning. Do numbers 1 through 6 just as you did Sample A. Darken the circle beside the correct answer.

Answers: Page 43

Sample A: lift it, **1.** pick, **2.** snowstorm, **3.** yell, **4.** smallest, **5.** bucket, **6.** ahead

Page 44

Say: Look at Sample A. Read the sentence in the box and the question below it: "Have you ever seen a two-dollar bill?" In which sentence does *bill* have the same meaning as it does in the sentence in the box? "I paid with two quarters and one dollar bill. ...Uncle Carl got a bill for the newspaper. ...A parrot has a big bill. ...The store will bill us for these shoes." Darken the circle beside the sentence that uses the word *bill* in the same way as the sentence in the box.

Say: Now you will finish the test on your own. Do numbers 1 through 17 just as you did Sample A. Read each selection carefully. Then darken the circle for each correct answer, or write in your answer.

Answers: Pages 39–42

Sample A: clean her room, **1.** water the seeds, **2.** Read a book about gardening., **3.** seeds, **4.** Possible answer: in the sun, **5.** about different kinds of owls, **6.** tell about a kind of bird, **7.** quietly, **8.** Possible answer: They have big eyes., **9.** all day, **10.** birds singing, **11.** Possible answer: tell someone at camp about his adventure, **12.** John's adventure in a cave, **13.** He wanted to see what was inside the cave., **14.** John got lost in a cave., **15.** frightened, **16.** true story, **17.** "John's Surprise"

Say: Look at **Think It Through**. The correct answer is the first sentence: "I paid with two quarters and one dollar bill." In this sentence and the sentence in the box, *bill* means "a type of money."

Say: Now you will practice matching more words that have more than one meaning. Do numbers 1 and 2 just as you did Sample A. Darken the circle beside the correct answer, or write in your answer.

Answers: Page 44

Sample A: I paid with two quarters and one dollar bill., **1.** The light from the flashlight helped us to see., **2.** Possible answer: She will ring the doorbell.

Page 45

Say: Look at Sample A. Read the sentence and the four answer choices: "The magician made the rabbit vanish from our sight. *Vanish* means — jump ...shine ...disappear ...smile." Darken the circle beside the word that has the same or almost the same meaning as the underlined word, *vanish*.

Say: Look at **Think It Through**. The correct answer is the third choice, "disappear." *Vanish* means "to no longer be seen." All four choices are things a magician could make a rabbit do. But only *disappear* has the same meaning as *vanish*.

Say: Now you will practice using clue words to figure out the meaning of more words. Do numbers 1 through 4 just as you did Sample A. Darken the circle beside the correct answer, or write in your answer.

Sample A: disappear, **1.** Possible answer: not allowed, **2.** drawing, **3.** keep, **4.** pushed

Page 46

Say: Put your finger under the first group of words. This is Sample A. Look at the words *carrot*, *harbor*, and *herself*. Which of these words is made up of two words put together? Darken the circle under the compound word.

Say: Look at **Think It Through**. The correct answer is the third choice, "herself." *Herself* is a compound word made up of the words *her* and *self*. Each of these words can stand alone. *Harbor* and *carrot* are not made up of two words put together.

Say: Now you will practice finding more compound words. Do numbers 1 through 8 just as you did Sample A. Darken the circle under the correct answer.

Answers: Page 46

Sample A: herself, **1.** mailbox, **2.** airplane, **3.** football, **4.** outside, **5.** anyway, **6.** someone, **7.** bedroom, **8.** bluebird

Page 47

Say: Look at Sample A. Look at the words *jumps… jumping…jumped*. These words are similar, but they do not have the same endings. Listen carefully as I say a word and use it in a sentence. You will find the word I say. Darken the circle under the word *jumped*. We *jumped* across the creek. *Jumped*.

Say: Look at **Think It Through**. The correct answer is the third word: "jumped." Although the word *jump* is a part of each word, *jumped* is the word that you heard.

Say: Now you will practice matching more printed words with words that you hear. Do numbers 1 through 8 just as you did Sample A. Listen carefully to the word and the sentence. Then darken the circle under the correct answer.

1. Darken the circle under the word *paints*. Her aunt *paints* beautifully. *Paints*.

2. Darken the circle under the word *quit*. Connie kept trying and would not *quit*. *Quit*.

3. Darken the circle under the word *careless*. Please don't be *careless* with your money. *Careless*.

4. Darken the circle under the word *nearly*. Paul *nearly* missed the bus. *Nearly*.

5. Darken the circle under the word *reading*. What are you *reading*? *Reading*.

6. Darken the circle under the word *sweeter*. A rose smells *sweeter* than grass. *Sweeter*.

7. Darken the circle under the word *harder*. Steel is *harder* than wood. *Harder*.

8. Darken the circle under the word *nicest*. This is the *nicest* gift I have ever received. *Nicest*.

Answers: Page 47

Sample A: jumped, **1.** paints, **2.** quit, **3.** careless, **4.** nearly, **5.** reading, **6.** sweeter, **7.** harder, **8.** nicest

Page 48

Say: Put your finger under the first group of words. This is Sample A. Look at the words *haven't… hadn't…hasn't*. Each of these words is a shortened form, or a contraction, of two other words. I will say two words and use them in a sentence. You will find the contraction that has the same meaning as the two words I say. Darken the circle under the word that means *have not*. I *have not* gone there. *Have not*.

Say: Look at **Think It Through**. The correct answer is the first word: "haven't." The contraction *haven't* means "have not." The sentence "I have not gone there" has the same meaning as the sentence "I haven't gone there." *Hadn't* means "had not," and *hasn't* means "has not."

Say: Now you will practice finding more contractions. Do numbers 1 through 8 just as you did Sample A. Listen carefully to the two words and the sentence. Then darken the circle under the correct answer.

1. Darken the circle under the word that means *we have*. *We have* been chosen the leaders. *We have*.

2. Move to the next group of words. Darken the circle under the word that means *will not*. We *will not* play if it's raining. *Will not*.

3. Move to the next group of words. Darken the circle under the word that means *do not*. I *do not* like storms. *Do not*.

4. Move to the next group of words. Darken the circle under the word that means *they are*. *They are* on vacation. *They are*.

5. Move to the next group of words. Darken the circle under the word that means *who would*. *Who would* like to sign up now? *Who would*.

6. Move to the next group of words. Darken the circle under the word that means *he will*. *He will* be next. *He will*.

7. Move to the next group of words. Darken the circle under the word that means *he is*. *He is* our neighbor. *He is*.

8. Move to the last group of words. Darken the circle under the word that means *you had*. *You had* better get dressed now. *You had*.

Answers: Page 48

Sample A: haven't, **1.** we've, **2.** won't, **3.** don't, **4.** they're, **5.** who'd, **6.** he'll, **7.** he's, **8.** you'd

Page 49

Say: Put your finger under the first group of words. This is Sample A. Look at the word *nose* and the three answer choices. Notice that the *o* in *nose* is underlined. Decide how the underlined part of the word sounds. Look at the three answer choices. Then darken the circle under the word that has the same sound as the underlined *o* in *nose*...*nose*.

Say: Look at **Think It Through**. The correct answer is the first word: "low." The *o* in *low* makes the same sound as the *o* in *nose*.

Say: Now you will practice matching more words that have the same sound or sounds. Do numbers 1 through 8 just as you did Sample A. Look at the first word in each row and say it silently to yourself. Say the three answer choices. Then darken the circle under the correct answer.

Answers: Page 49

Sample A: low **1.** this, **2.** cow, **3.** writing, **4.** wilt, **5.** noon, **6.** fair, **7.** kitten, **8.** fast

Test, part 1: Pages 50–51

Say: Turn to the Test on page 50. This test is divided into three parts. For each part there is a sample exercise. We will work each sample together. Look at Sample A. In this part of the test, you will find words that have the same or almost the same meanings. Read the sentence and the four answer choices: "A command is a kind of — order ...boat ...test ...question." Darken the circle beside the word that has the same or almost the same meaning as the underlined word, *command*.

Say: The correct answer is the first word, "order." *Command* and *order* have the same meaning.

Say: Now you will finish this part of the test on your own. Do numbers 1 through 4 in the first column just as you did Sample A. Darken the circle beside the correct answer.

Say: Now find Sample B at the top of the second column on page 50. In this part of the test, you will match words that have more than one meaning. Look at Sample B. In which sentence does the word *time* have the same meaning as it does in the sentence: "What time does the show start?" Is it ...I will time my brother's race. ...We

kept time with the music. ...Everyone had a good time. ...It's time for lunch.? Darken the circle beside the sentence that uses the word *time* in the same way as the sentence in the box.

Say: The correct answer is the fourth sentence: "It's time for lunch." In this sentence and in the sentence in the box, the word *time* means "when something takes place."

Say: Now you will match more words that have more than one meaning. Do numbers 5 through 9 just as you did Sample B. Darken the circle beside the correct answer, or write in your answer.

Say: Now find Sample C at the top of the second column on page 51. In the last part of the test, you will use clue words to help you figure out the meaning of underlined words. Look at Sample C. "The two people yelling argue about everything. *To argue* means to — fight ...plan ...sing ...read." Darken the circle for the word that gives the meaning of the underlined word, *argue*.

Say: The correct answer is the first word, "fight." *Fight* means the same as *argue*.

Say: Now you will finish this part of the test on your own. Do numbers 10 through 12 just as you did Sample C. Darken the circle beside the correct answer.

Answers: Pages 50–51

Sample A: order, **1.** barely, **2.** start, **3.** bunch, **4.** shines, **Sample B:** It's time for lunch., **5.** Please wipe up the drop of paint., **6.** The box was tied with string., **7.** Tim found the key to solving the puzzle., **8.** Possible answer: I visited my aunt last week., **9.** The iron horseshoe is strong., **Sample C:** fight, **10.** design, **11.** empty, **12.** bright

Test, part 2: Pages 52–53

Say: Turn to page 52. Now you will use the word study skills we have practiced in this unit. This test is divided into four parts. For each part there is a sample exercise. We will work each sample together. In the first part of the test, you will find compound words. Put your finger under Sample A. Look at the words *postcard*, *eleven*, and *pilot*. Which of the three words is made of two words put together? Darken the circle under the compound word.

Say: The correct answer is the first word: "postcard." *Postcard* is a compound word made up of the words *post* and *card*.

Say: Now you will find more compound words. Do numbers 1 through 6 just as you did Sample A. Darken the circle under the correct answer.

Say: Now go to the top of the second column and find Sample B. In this part of the test, you will match printed words with words that you hear. Look at the words *neatly ...neatest ...neater*. Listen carefully as I say a word and use it in a sentence.

Darken the circle under the word *neatest*. This is the *neatest* I have ever seen your room. *Neatest*.

Say: The correct answer is the second word, "neatest." *Neat* is a part of all the words, but *neatest* is the word you heard.

Say: Now you will choose more words that you hear. Do numbers 7 through 12 just as you did Sample B. Listen carefully to the word and the sentence. Then darken the circle under the correct answer.

7. Darken the circle under the word *slower*. It is *slower* to travel by car than by plane. *Slower*.

8. Move to the next group of words. Darken the circle under the word *called*. We *called* Grandma long distance. *Called*.

9. Move to the next group of words. Darken the circle under the word *helper*. Dad will need a *helper*. *Helper*.

10. Move to the next group of words. Darken the circle under the word *folded*. Tanya *folded* the clean laundry. *Folded*.

11. Move to the next group of words. Darken the circle under the word *clearly*. I could see myself *clearly* in the pond. *Clearly*.

12. Move to the last group of words. Darken the circle under the word *locked*. We made sure the door was *locked*. *Locked*.

Say: Now turn to page 53 and find Sample C. In this part of the test, you will find contractions. Look at the words *we've ...we're ...we'd*. Each of these words is a contraction. I will say two words and use them in a sentence. You will find the contraction that has the same meaning as the two words I say. Darken the circle under the word that means *we are*. *We are* having fun. *We are*.

Say: The correct answer is the second word: "we're." *We're* is the contraction of the words *we are*.

Say: Now you will find more contractions. Do numbers 13 through 18 just as you did Sample C. Listen carefully to the two words and the sentence. Then darken the circle under the correct answer.

13. Darken the circle under the word that means *it is*. *It is* rainy today. *It is*.

14. Move to the next group of words. Darken the circle under the word that means *had not*. Julie *had not* yet received her card. *Had not*.

15. Move to the next group of words. Darken the circle under the word that means *you would*. *You would* play. *You would*.

16. Move to the next group of words. Darken the circle under the word that means *would not*. Ben *would not* leave until the job was done. *Would not*.

17. Move to the next group of words. Darken the circle under the word that means *where is*. *Where is* the paintbrush? *Where is*.

18. Move to the last group of words. Darken the circle under the word that means *I have*. *I have* been here before. *I have*.

Say: Now find Sample D at the top of the second column. In the last part of the test, you will match printed words that have the same sound or sounds. Look at the word *wish* and the three answer choices. Notice that the *sh* in *wish* is underlined. Decide how the underlined part of the word sounds. Then darken the circle under the word that has the same sound as the underlined *sh* in *wish*.

Say: The correct answer is the first word, "shop." *Shop* has the same sound as the *sh* in *wish*.

Say: Now you will practice matching more words that have the same sound or sounds. Do numbers 19 through 24 just as you did Sample D. Look at the first word in each row and say it silently to yourself. Say the three answer choices. Then darken the circle under the correct answer.

Answers: Pages 52–53

Sample A: postcard, 1. raincoat, 2. notebook, 3. bathtub, 4. upstairs, 5. birthday, 6. sidewalk, **Sample B:** neatest, 7. slower, 8. called, 9. helper, 10. folded, 11. clearly, 12. locked, **Sample C:** we're, 13. it's, 14. hadn't, 15. you'd, 16. wouldn't, 17. where's, 18. I've, **Sample D:** shop, 19. chip, 20. loose, 21. tie, 22. mop, 23. apple, 24. grow

Unit 5

Answers: Page 55

Step 1: How much did Paul pay for 3 apples?

Step 2: 1st apple 25¢; additional apples 20¢ each

Step 3: compute

Step 4: 25 + 20 + 20 = 65; all 3 apples cost 65¢

Step 5: yes

Answers: Page 56

Step 1: to find the number Jenny is thinking about

Step 2: The number is less than 9. The number is greater than 5. The number is odd.

Step 3: Use logical thinking.

Step 4: The numbers that are more than 5 and less than 9 are 6, 7, 8. The only odd number is 7. Jenny is thinking of the number 7.

Step 5: yes

Unit 6

Page 57

Say: You will practice choosing pictures and numbers that answer math problems. Place your finger under the first row. Look at the numbers. This is Sample A. Now listen carefully. Darken the circle under the number that shows the correct way to write *three hundred plus fifty*.

Say: Now look at **Think It Through**. The correct answer is the third number, 350. This is the only number that equals 300 + 50.

Say: Now you will practice choosing more pictures and numbers that answer math problems. Do numbers 1 through 3 just as you did Sample A. Listen carefully to each problem. For number 1, write in your answer. For numbers 2 and 3, choose your answer from the pictures or numbers given for the problem.

Say:

1. Place your finger under the row for number 1. Write the number that is in the hundreds place.

2. Move to the next row. Katya plays baseball. She wears a baseball shirt with an even number. Darken the circle under the picture of Katya's baseball shirt.

3. Move to the last row. Darken the circle under the number that tells how many carrots are shown in the picture.

Answers: Page 57

Sample A: 350, **1.** nine, **2.** shirt with number 6 on it, **3.** 57

Page 58

Say: You will practice choosing pictures and numbers that answer math problems about whole numbers, fractions, and decimals. Place your finger under the first row. Look at the four shapes. This is Sample A. Now listen carefully. Darken the circle under the shape that is not divided into fourths.

Say: Now look at **Think It Through**. The correct answer is the third shape. All the other shapes are divided into fourths.

Say: Now you will practice choosing more pictures and numbers that answer math problems about whole numbers, fractions, and decimals. Do numbers 1 through 4 just as you did Sample A. Listen carefully to each problem. Then choose your answer from the pictures or numbers given for the problem, or write in your answer.

Say:

1. The number sentence *eight minus two* describes this picture. Darken the circle under another number sentence that also describes this picture.

2. Move to the next row. Darken the circle under the picture that shows that one third of the apples have been eaten.

3. Move to the next row. Write the number that belongs in the box to make the number sentence correct.

4. Move to the last row. Darken the circle under the number that belongs in the box to make the number sentence correct.

Answers: Page 58

Sample A: third shape, **1.** 6 + 2 = 8, **2.** first group of apples, **3.** 0, **4.** 21

Page 59

Say: You will practice choosing pictures and numbers that answer math problems about numbers and patterns. Place your finger under the first row, the one with the numbers on the doors. This is Sample A. These numbers make a pattern. Darken the circle under the number that is missing in the pattern.

Say: Now look at **Think It Through**. The correct answer is 15. Each of the numbers is 3 greater than the one before it. $12 + 3 = 15$, so this is the missing number.

Say: Now you will practice choosing more pictures and numbers that answer math problems about numbers and patterns. Do numbers 1 through 3 just as you did Sample A. Listen carefully to each problem. Then choose your answer from the pictures or numbers given for the problem, or write in your answer.

Say:

1. Look at the pattern of squares and triangles. Darken the circle under the two shapes that come next in the pattern.

2. Move to the next row. Look at the numbers in the boxes. These numbers make a pattern. Write the number that is missing in the pattern.

3. Move to the last row. Ms. Burrus took a nature walk. She counted the birds she saw. She counted 62, 63, 64. Darken the circle under the bird that would be counted number 71.

Answers: Page 59

Sample A: 15, **1.** third group, **2.** 25, **3.** second circle should be darkened

Page 60

Say: You will practice choosing numbers and pictures that answer math problems about graphs, charts, and simple probability. Place your finger under the first row, the one with the tally chart. This is Sample A. The chart shows the numbers and kinds of shells Ann found while walking on the beach. Darken the circle under the picture of the shell that Ann found six of.

Say: Now look at **Think It Through**. The correct answer is the whelk. If you count the tally marks, Ann found 6 whelk shells.

Say: Now you will practice choosing more pictures and numbers that answer math problems about graphs, charts, and simple probability. Do numbers 1 and 2 just as you did Sample A. Listen

carefully to each problem. Then choose your answer from the pictures or numbers given for the problem, or write in your answer.

Say:

1. Look at the the graph titled "Soccer Points." The graph shows the points scored in a soccer game. Write the number that shows how many points Joe scored.

2. Move to the last row. Ivan is playing a game with the spinner. He spins the dial 100 times. Darken the circle under the shape that the spinner most likely will land on the greatest number of times.

Answers: Page 60

Sample A: whelk, **1.** 3, **2.** fourth shape, the pentagon

Page 61

Say: You will practice choosing pictures that answer math problems about shapes. Place your finger under the first row. This is Sample A. Darken the circle under the shape whose parts will match exactly when it is folded along the dotted line.

Say: Now look at **Think It Through**. The correct answer is the third shape. If you fold this figure on the dotted line, each side will be the same.

Say: Now you will practice choosing more pictures that answer math problems about shapes. Do numbers 1 through 3 just as you did Sample A. Listen carefully to each problem. Then choose your answer from the pictures given for the problem.

Say:

1. Look at the shapes in the boxes. Now listen carefully. Darken the circle under the box that has two triangles.

2. Move to the next row. Look at the shape at the beginning of the row. Darken the circle under the shape that has the same number of sides as the one at the beginning of the row.

3. Move to the last row. Look at the first picture in the row. Sonya made this card. She turned it upside down. Darken the circle under the picture that shows what the card looks like upside down.

Answers: Page 61

Sample A: third figure, **1.** fourth figure, **2.** second figure, **3.** second figure

Page 62

Say: You will practice choosing pictures and numbers that answer math problems about measurement. Place your finger under the first row, the one with the picture of the coins. This is Sample A. Sue has these coins. She wants to buy the banana. Darken the circle under the number that tells the amount of money that Sue will have left.

Say: Now look at **Think It Through**. The correct answer is 15¢. Sue has 28¢. The banana costs 13¢. To find out how much Sue gets back, subtract 13¢ from 28¢. This gives you the answer, 15¢.

Say: Now you will practice finding more pictures and numbers that answer math problems about measurement. Do numbers 1 through 3 just as you did Sample A. Listen carefully to each problem. Then choose your answer from the pictures or numbers given for the problem, or write in your answer.

Say:

1. Use your centimeter ruler to measure the key. Write the number that tells how many centimeters long the key is.

2. Move to the next row. Darken the circle under the measurement unit that is best to use to measure the weight of a dog.

3. Move to the last row. Darken the circle next to the day that is August 13 on the calendar.

Answers: Page 62

Sample A: 15¢, **1.** 7 centimeters, **2.** pounds, **3.** Monday

Page 63

Say: You will practice choosing numbers and number sentences that answer word problems you hear. Place your finger under the first row. This is Sample A. Mrs. Chong bought 12 flowers. She put 8 of the flowers in a vase. Which number sentence shows how to find the number of flowers that Mrs. Chong has left? Darken the circle under the number sentence that shows how to find the number of flowers Mrs. Chong has left.

Say: Now look at **Think It Through**. The correct answer is $12 - 8$. The clue words, "has left," tell you to subtract. Mrs. Chong has 12 flowers and puts 8 in a vase, so $12 - 8$ is the number sentence that answers the question.

Say: Now you will practice choosing more numbers and number sentences that answer math problems you hear. Do numbers 1 through 4 just as you did Sample A. Listen carefully to each problem. Then choose your answer from the number sentences and numbers given for the problem, or write in your answer.

Say:

1. Nathan had 3 fish. He bought 9 more fish. Which number sentence shows how to find the number of fish Nathan had altogether? Darken the circle under the number sentence that shows how to find the number of fish Nathan had altogether.

2. Move to the next row. Listen to this riddle. I am a number less than 35. The sum of my digits is 11. What number am I? Darken the circle for the number that answers the riddle.

3. Move to the next row. Listen to this riddle. My aunt's age is between 31 and 41. It is less than 34. The sum of my digits is 5. What number am I? Write the number that answers the riddle.

4. Move to the last row. Listen to this riddle. I am a number inside the square and inside the triangle. I am an even number. What number am I? Darken the circle for the number that answers the riddle.

Answers: Page 63

Sample A: $12 - 8 =$, **1.** $3 + 9 =$, **2.** 29, **3.** 32, **4.** 2

Pages 64–65

Say: You will practice adding and subtracting numbers to answer word problems you hear. Place your finger under the first row, the one with the picture of the presents. This is Sample A. Look at the answer choices in Sample A. In some problems you will find that the correct answer is not given among the answer choices. When that happens, darken the circle for NH, which means *Not Here*. Listen carefully to this story. It is Soon-Li's birthday. She receives 9 presents from her friends. She receives 5 presents from her family. How many presents does she receive altogether? Darken the circle for the number that tells how many presents Soon-Li receives altogether.

Say: Now look at **Think It Through**. The correct answer is the third choice: 14. She gets 9 presents from her friends and 5 presents from her family. The word *altogether* tells you to add. So there are 14 presents altogether, because $9 + 5 = 14$.

Say: Now you will practice adding and subtracting more numbers that answer word problems you hear. Do numbers 1 through 14 just as you did Sample A. Listen carefully to each problem. Then darken the circle for the correct answer, or write in the answer. If you add or subtract a problem and find that the answer is not among the answer choices, darken the circle for NH for Not Here. (Say each item only once.)

Say:

1. Place your finger under the row for number 1. An art gallery has 60 pictures on the first floor. There are 34 pictures on the second floor. How many pictures are in the art gallery in all? Darken the circle for the number that tells how many pictures are in the art gallery in all.

2. Move to the row for number 2. There were 5 sailboats on the lake. Then 3 more sailboats joined them. How many sailboats were on the lake altogether? Darken the circle under the number that tells how many sailboats were on the lake altogether.

3. Move to the row for number 3. The school cafeteria workers served soup for lunch. They served 56 bowls of chicken noodle soup. They served 24 bowls of vegetable soup. How many bowls of soup did they serve altogether? Darken the circle for the number that tells how many bowls of soup the school cafeteria workers served altogether.

4. Move to the row for number 4. Mrs. Logan took her class on a weekend trip to the space center. Eighteen students had large suitcases. Seven students had small suitcases. How many suitcases were there altogether? Write in the number that tells how many suitcases there were altogether.

Say: Go on to the top of the next page.

5. Move to the row for number 5. Jesse counted 55 cocoons in his garden. He saw that butterflies came out of 23 cocoons. How many cocoons are left? Darken the circle under the number that tells how many cocoons are left.

6. Move to the row for number 6. The hardware store has 26 padlocks and 9 key locks. How many more padlocks does the store have? Darken the circle under the number that tells how many more padlocks than key locks the store has.

7. Move to the row for number 7. There were 53 winner's ribbons to present at the county dog show. The judges presented 23 ribbons this morning. How many ribbons are left to present this afternoon? Darken the circle for the number of ribbons that are left to present.

8. Move to the row for number 8. The garden center received a shipment of 123 potted plants this morning. One of the workers unpacked 47 of the plants. How many plants are left to unpack? Darken the circle for the number of plants that still need to be unpacked.

9. Move to the row for number 9. A pizza restaurant sold 41 sausage and mushroom pizzas. It sold 12 plain mushroom pizzas. How many more sausage and mushroom pizzas did the pizza restaurant sell? Darken the circle under the number that tells how many more sausage and mushroom pizzas than plain mushroom pizzas the restaurant sold.

10. Move to the row for number 10. Look at the pictures of the clowns. Twelve circus clowns wear hats that are round on the top. Nine circus clowns wear hats that are pointed on the top. How many more clowns wear round hats than pointed hats? Darken the circle for the number that tells how many more clowns wear round hats than pointed hats.

11. Move to the row for number 11. The staff at Fire Station 9 collected 207 toys to distribute to children in the county hospital. They have already distributed 66 of the toys. How many toys are left? Darken the circle for the number of toys that still need to be distributed.

12. Move to the row for number 12. Mr. Ardjani owns an ice cream store. On Monday, he sold 82 ice cream cones. He sold 47 sundaes the same day. How many more cones than sundaes did he sell? Darken the circle under the number that tells how many more cones than sundaes Mr. Ardjani sold on Monday.

13. Move to the row for number 13. Ms. Elda sells cars and trucks. She sold 126 cars in one year. She also sold 71 trucks that same year. How many cars and trucks did Ms. Elda sell altogether? Write the number that tells how many cars and trucks Ms. Elda sold altogether.

14. Move to the last row on the page for number 14. Jacob has a herd of goats. He has 30 brown goats and 16 white goats. How many more brown goats are there? Darken the circle under the number that tells how many more brown goats than white goats Jacob has.

Answers: Pages 64–65

Sample A: 14, **1.** 94, **2.** 8, **3.** 80, **4.** 25, **5.** 32, **6.** 17, **7.** NH, **8.** 76, **9.** 29, **10.** 3, **11.** 141, **12.** 35, **13.** 197, **14.** 14

Page 66

Say: You will practice adding and subtracting numbers to find the answers to math problems that you read. Place your finger under the first row. This is Sample A. Look at the answer choices. In some problems the correct answer is not given among the answer choices. When that happens, darken the circle for

NH, which means *Not Here*. Now listen carefully. You are asked to subtract 9 from 17. Work the problem. Then darken the circle for the correct answer. Darken the circle for NH if the answer is not given.

Say: Now look at **Think It Through**. The correct answer is the second choice: 8. $17 - 9 = 8$. The second answer choice is correct because you can check your answer by adding the 9 and the 8, which gives you 17.

Say: Now you will practice adding and subtracting more numbers that you read. Do problems 1 through 6 on your own. Read each problem carefully. Use the scratch paper to work the problem. Then darken the circle for the correct answer, or write in your answer. If you find that the answer is not among the answer choices, darken the circle for NH. (Allow the child time to choose and mark the answers.)

Answers: Page 66
Sample A: 8, **1.** 472, **2.** 5, **3.** 16, **4.** 37, **5.** NH, **6.** 34

Test, part 1: Pages 67–68

Say: In this test you will add or subtract numbers that answer math problems you hear or read. Place your finger under the first row, the one with the pictures of the people. This is Sample A. The Oak Hill neighborhood is having a neighborhood work day. One hundred forty-six people clean up the trash around the neighborhood. Forty-two people plant trees and shrubs. How many people in the neighborhood took part in the neighborhood work day? Darken the circle under the number that tells how many people in the neighborhood took part in neighborhood work day.

Say: The correct answer is the third choice, 188. When you add 146 and 42, the answer is 188.

Say: Now move to the next row. This is Sample B. Ada makes necklaces. She used 46 round beads and 25 long beads on a necklace. How many more round beads than long beads did Ada use? Darken the circle under the number that tells how many more round beads than long beads Ada used to make the necklace.

Say: The correct answer is the first choice, 21. $46 - 25 = 21$.

Say: In the first part of the test, you will add or subtract more numbers to find the answers to math problems you hear. Listen carefully to each problem. Then darken the circle for the correct answer. Darken the circle for NH if the correct answer is not given. (Say each item only once.)

Say:

1. Place your finger under the row for number 1. There were 13 bees on a patch of clover. Then 6 of the bees flew away. How many bees were left? Darken the circle under the number that tells how many bees were left.

2. Move to the row for number 2. Mr. Becker is making pies and muffins for a bake sale. He buys 27 apples to make the pies. He buys 8 apples to make the muffins. How many apples does Mr. Becker buy in all? Write in the number that tells how many apples Mr. Becker buys in all.

3. Move to the row for number 3. Anton went to the zoo with his class. He saw 8 giraffes in the morning. He saw 3 giraffes in the afternoon. How many more giraffes did he see in the morning? Darken the circle under the number that tells how many more giraffes Anton saw in the morning than in the afternoon.

4. Move to the row for number 4. Jackie cleaned 9 shells that she collected on the beach. She found that 4 of the shells were too cracked to save, and she threw them away. How many shells did Jackie have left? Darken the circle for the number of shells Jackie had left.

5. Move to the row for number 5. Keesha grows roses. She counted 32 red roses. She counted 16 yellow roses. How many roses does Keesha have altogether? Darken the circle under the number that tells how many roses Keesha has altogether.

6. Move to the row for number 6. You are asked to add 7 and 5. Use some scratch paper and work the problem. Darken the circle for the correct answer. If the correct answer is not shown, darken the circle for NH for Not Here.

7. Move to the row for number 7. Ramón works at a hot dog stand. Today he cooked 80 hot dogs. He sold 67 of the hot dogs. How many hot dogs does Ramón have left? Darken the circle under the number that tells how many hot dogs are left.

8. Move to the last row for number 8. My cousin Bob has been collecting comic books for about 10 years. He had 614 comic books. Last month he went to a book show and he bought 44 more comic books. How many comic books does he have in his collection now? Darken the circle for the number of comic books Bob has in his collection altogether.

Say: Now go to the top of page 68. In the last part of the test, you will practice adding and subtracting numbers that answer math problems you read. Do numbers 9 through 18 on your own, just as you did Sample B. Read the problem carefully. Use scratch paper to work the problem. Then darken the circle for the correct answer, or write in the answer. If the correct answer is not given, darken the circle for NH for Not Here.

Answers: Pages 67–68

Sample A: 188, **Sample B:** 21, **1.** 7, **2.** 35, **3.** NH, **4.** NH, **5.** 48, **6.** 12, **7.** NH, **8.** 658, **9.** 6, **10.** 59, **11.** 84, **12.** 48, **13.** 26, **14.** 405, **15.** 3, **16.** 37, **17.** 561, **18.** NH

Test, part 2: Pages 69–73

Say: In this test you will choose pictures and numbers that answer math problems you hear. Place your finger under the first row. This is Sample A. The number sentence 4 plus 1 describes this picture. Darken the circle under another number sentence that also describes this picture.

Say: The correct answer is the last number sentence, $5 - 1 = 4$. The picture shows 5 apples with 1 apple taken away. This leaves 4 apples on the plate.

Say: Now you will choose more pictures and numbers that answer math problems you hear. Do numbers 1 through 26 just as you did Sample A. Listen carefully to each problem. Then choose your answer from the pictures or numbers given for the problem. (Say each item only once.)

Say:

1. Place your finger under the row for number 1. Darken the circle under the number that is between 72 and 95.

2. Move to the next row. Darken the circle under the number that is in the ones place.

3. Move to the next row. Darken the circle under the number that names the greatest amount.

4. Move to the next row. Darken the circle under the number 692.

5. Move to the last row. Write the number that is 100 more than 538.

Say: Now go to the top of page 70.

6. Place your finger under the first row. Look at the numbers in the circles. These numbers make a pattern. Write the number that is missing in the pattern.

7. Move to the next row. Darken the circle under the number that goes in the box to make the number sentence correct.

8. Move to the next row. Look at the team shirts. Listen carefully. Marta was helping pass out the new team shirts. She counts to see how many shirts she has. She counts 13, 14, 15. Darken the circle under the shirt that would be 22.

9. Move to the next row. Darken the circle under the fraction that tells what part of the triangle is shaded.

10. Move to the last row. Darken the circle under the group of buttons that shows one quarter shaded.

Say: Now go to the top of page 71.

11. Place your finger under the row for number 11. Look at the chart. Darken the circle under the name of the tallest child.

12. Move to the next row. Darken the circle under the shape that comes next in the pattern.

Say: Look at the graph titled "Animal Tracks." The graph shows the number and kinds of tracks that Mr. Garza's class saw on their nature walk. Use this graph to answer numbers 13 and 14.

13. Move to the row for number 13. Darken the circle under the name of the animal that left the fewest number of tracks.

14. Move to the last row. Write the number that tells how many fox tracks the class counted.

Say: Now go to the top of page 72.

15. Place your finger under the row for number 15. Look at the clocks. The clocks show the time that Inga starts and stops her piano lesson. Write the time that tells how long Inga's lesson lasts.

16. Move to the next row. Darken the circle under the shape that can be folded on the dotted line and the parts will not match exactly.

17. Move to the next row. Look at the card at the beginning of the row. Fred cut a shape from this card. Darken the circle under the picture that shows the shape that was cut from the card.

18. Move to the next row. Use your inch ruler to measure the toy bus. Darken the circle under the number that tells how many inches long the toy bus is from one end to the other.

19. Move to the next row. If Alice picks a card without looking, which card will she most likely pick? Darken the circle under the letter of the card Alice will pick.

20. Move to the last row. Darken the circle under the longest piece of chalk.

Say: Now go to the top of page 73.

21. Place your finger under the row for number 21. Look at the picture of the coins. Darken the circle under the number that shows the value of the coins.

22. Move to the next row. Miguel made a spinner for a game. He spins it many times. Write the name of the month that the spinner will land on the fewest number of times.

23. Move to the next row. Darken the circle under the unit of measurement that is best to use to measure the amount of juice in a jar.

24. Move to the next row. Listen to this riddle. I am an odd number inside the square and outside the circle. What number am I? Darken the circle for the number that answers the riddle.

25. Move to the next row. Listen to this riddle. I am a number between 20 and 30. The sum of my digits is 8. What number am I? Darken the circle for the number that answers the riddle.

26. Move to the last row. Listen to this story. Sixteen children are on the bus. Five more children get on the bus. Which number sentence shows how to find the number of children on the bus altogether? Darken the circle under the number sentence that shows how to find the number of children on the bus altogether.

Answers: Pages 69–73

Sample A: $5 - 1 = 4$, **1.** 89, **2.** 4, **3.** 314, **4.** 692, **5.** 638, **6.** 80, **7.** 17, **8.** the second circle should be darkened, **9.** $\frac{1}{2}$, **10.** third figure, **11.** Anna, **12.** second figure, **13.** raccoon, **14.** 6, **15.** 30 minutes, **16.** fourth figure, **17.** third figure, **18.** 2, **19.** D, **20.** first figure, **21.** 15¢, **22.** May, **23.** ounces, **24.** 11, **25.** 26, **26.** $16 + 5$

Unit 7

Page 74

Say: You will practice choosing words that best complete sentences. Look at Sample A. I will read part of a sentence and three words. You will find the word that best completes the sentence. Will came in the door wearing a big grin. A grin is a ...pair of shorts ...smile ...new haircut. Darken the circle for the correct answer.

Say: Now look at **Think It Through**. The correct answer is "smile." *To grin* means the same thing as to *smile*.

Say: Now you will practice choosing more words that best complete sentences. Do numbers 1 through 8 just as you did Sample A. Listen carefully to the sentences and the three answer choices. Then darken the circle for the correct answer.

Say:

1. That pipe is leaking water. When something is leaking, it is ...dripping ...screaming ...breaking.

2. Move to the next row. The deer fled through the forest. *Fled* means ...walked ...ran away ... wandered.

3. Move to the next row. Autumn is my favorite time of year. Another word for autumn is ...summer ... fall ...winter.

4. Move to the next row. Michael advanced to the front of the line. *To advance* means to ...move forward ...move backward ...move beyond.

5. Move to the next row. Kayla and Alex visited the seashore. *Seashore* means the same as ...forest ... beach ...library.

6. Move to the next row. Hannah suddenly started sneezing. *Suddenly* means ...without warning ...after a long time ...in a mad way.

7. Move to the next row. My parents expect me to do well in school. To expect is to ...think something will happen ...look at something very well ...give a reward.

8. Move to the last row. Mr. Stevens had a grim expression on his face. *Grim* means the same as ...silly ...gloomy ...clever.

Answers: Page 74

Sample A: smile, **1.** dripping, **2.** ran away, **3.** fall, **4.** move forward, **5.** beach, **6.** without warning, **7.** think something will happen, **8.** gloomy

Page 75

Say: You will practice choosing pictures that best answer questions. Place your finger under the first row. This is Sample A. I will read a story and then ask a question. You will find the picture that best answers the question. Listen carefully. It was Saturday and it was raining. Mei could not go out to play with her friends. After she ate lunch, Mei told her mother, "I have nothing to do. What can I do that's fun?" Her mother asked, "Why don't you watch TV?" But Mei said she didn't want to watch TV. Then Mei's mother showed her a trunk filled with old clothes, purses, hats, and other things. Mei's mother said, "Here, use your imagination and have fun." How did Mei have fun on a rainy Saturday? Did she ...watch TV ... eat lunch ...play dress-up? Darken the circle for the correct answer.

Say: Now look at **Think It Through**. The correct answer is the third picture. Mei's mother gave her old clothes to play dress-up with.

Say: Now you will practice choosing more pictures that best answer questions. Do numbers 1 through 4 just as you did Sample A. Study the pictures, and listen carefully to the story and the question. Then darken the circle for the correct answer.

Say:

1. Listen to this story. On Saturday Mr. Ota did chores. First, he cleaned his house. Then, he fixed a broken window. Finally, he washed his car. Which is a chore Mr. Ota did on Saturday? Did he ...read the newspaper ...work in his garden ...clean his house? Darken the circle for the correct answer.

2. Move to the next row. Listen to the story. Jan asked her grandma what she could have for lunch. "Look in the refrigerator," said Grandma. "There is some leftover pizza." But Jan didn't want pizza. So Grandma fixed her something else. Jan said, "Thanks, Grandma. That looks good. My favorite part is the bun." What did Jan have for lunch? ...a hot dog ...a sandwich ...or pizza? Darken the circle for the picture that shows what Jan ate for lunch.

3. Move to the next row. Listen to this poem:

   "I'm late!" Daniel thought as he rushed to get dressed.

   "No time to finish, what will I do?"

   So he ran out the front door,

   Carrying his _____.

   Darken the circle for the picture that shows something that will rhyme with the poem.

4. Move to the next row. Listen to this story. Monica loved animals, but she didn't have a pet. So, she played with her friend's dog whenever she could. Monica also liked to visit her neighbor, Mrs. Reyna, who had a cat and a gerbil. Which animal did Monica play with at her friend's house? Was it ...a cat ...a dog ...or a gerbil?

Answers: Page 75

Sample A: third picture, **1.** third picture, **2.** first picture, **3.** third picture, **4.** second picture

Page 76

Say: You will practice choosing words that best answer questions about stories that you hear. Listen carefully. When I read a story, look at the words or phrases given in each row. Then darken the circle for the word or phrase that goes with the story. Now place your finger under the first row. This is Sample A. Listen to the story. You will answer one question. Every Saturday, Joseph helps his grandmother. He helps her do her grocery shopping. Then, he mows her lawn. Finally, after lunch, he sweeps the porch. What does Joseph do first on Saturdays to help his grandmother? Is it ...mows the lawn ...goes grocery shopping ...sweeps the porch?

Say: Now look at **Think It Through**. The correct answer is "goes grocery shopping." The story says that Joseph goes grocery shopping first.

Say: Now you will practice choosing more words that best answer questions about passages that you hear. Do numbers 1 through 8 just as you did Sample A. Listen to the passage and the questions. Then darken the circle for the correct answer for each question.

Say:

1. Listen to this poem. You will answer one question.

   Patty and Jonathan's favorite toy

   Is one that's good for a girl or a boy.

   It's fun to bounce and easy to throw,

   What is it? I'll bet you know!

   What toy is the poem about? Is it ...a kite ...a yoyo ...a ball?

2. Place your finger on number 2. Listen carefully to this poem:

   Gary said he wanted some cake.

   Mom said that was dandy,

   But she had no time to bake.

   Gary said, "Fine. I'll have some candy!"

   What kind of snack did Gary have? Was it ...cookies ...candy ...cake?

Say: Place your finger on number 3. Listen to these rules. You will answer two questions.

   Rules for the Petting Zoo:

   Rule 1. Do not bring food or drinks into the petting zoo.

   Rule 2. Do not shout or make loud noises.

   Rule 3. Be gentle with the animals.

Say:

3. A person carrying a soda into the petting zoo would probably ...disturb the animals ...be asked to leave ...have to pay extra.

4. According to the rules, people in the petting zoo should not ...shout ...talk ...pet the animals.

Say: Now put your finger on number 5. Listen as I read this story. You will answer two questions. In April, second-graders at Goodman School were learning about ways to help save planet Earth. On Earth Day, they had many activities. They visited a recycling plant. They made a list of ways to save water. They picked up trash in a park. They planted a tree on the school grounds. Finally, to end their special day, they saw a puppet show that reminded them of all the things they can do to help save planet Earth.

Say:

5. What was the last thing the second-graders did? Did they watch ...a talent show ...a magic show ...a puppet show?

6. What is a good title for the story? ..."An Earth Day Celebration" ..."How to Save Water" ..."A Fall Festival."

Say: Now put your finger on number 7. Listen as I read this passage. You will answer two questions. Texas is a great place to visit. When people go to Texas, they want to be sure to visit the Alamo. They like to see the site of a famous battle for independence. The Alamo is a favorite spot for visitors. But there are many other things to see and do in Texas. You could go to a rodeo, visit a ranch that was the home of a President, or even go to the beach on the Gulf of Mexico. You might want to try Texas for your next vacation.

Say:

7. What would be a good title for this passage? ..."View of the Grand Canyon" ..."Visiting A President's Ranch" ..."Seeing A Cattle Ranch" ...or "A Texas Tour"?

8. What is the favorite spot for visitors to Texas? Is it ...the beach ...the Alamo ...the state capital ...or Yellowstone National Park?

Answers: Page 76

Sample A: goes grocery shopping, **1.** a ball, **2.** candy, **3.** be asked to leave, **4.** shout, **5.** a puppet show, **6.** "An Earth Day Celebration", **7.** "A Texas Tour", **8.** the Alamo

Test: Pages 77–79

Say: In this test you will use the listening skills we have practiced in this unit. This test is divided into three parts. For each part there is a sample exercise. We will work each sample together. Look at Sample A. In this part of the test, you will choose the words that best complete sentences. I will read part of a sentence and three words. You will find the word that best completes the sentence. Mom gave each of us an additional snack. *Additional* means the same as ...extra ...whole ...special.

Say: The correct answer is "extra," because *additional* means almost the same as *extra*.

Say: Now you will find more words that best complete sentences. Do numbers 1 through 13 just as you did Sample A. Listen carefully to the sentence and the three answer choices. Darken the circle for the correct answer.

Say:

1. Jacob's father is the original owner of the store. Another word for original is ...last ...first ...next.

2. Mrs. Honeycutt wants us to compete in the relay race. *To compete* means to ...take part ...keep score ...watch.

3. What was your mom's reply to your question? A reply is ...an answer ...a report ...a picture.

4. Our campfire started to flare while we were cooking our food. *To flare* means to ...go out ...flicker ...blaze.

5. Can you pitch the ball to me? *To pitch* means to ...set down ...throw ...put away.

6. Jenny is uncertain about playing on a soccer team. *Uncertain* means not ...happy ...allowed ...sure.

7. Is there anything to nibble on? *To nibble* means to ...wash ...stack ...eat.

8. It is wise to value money. *To value* means to ...appreciate ...spend ...save.

9. After it rained, all the leaves on the trees glistened. *To glisten* means to ...blow ...shake ...shine.

10. My favorite time of day is twilight. *Twilight* means the time near ...sunset ...sunrise ...noon.

11. The man spoke to us in a gruff voice. *Gruff* means ...sad ...rough ...playful.

12. All the farmers were worried about the drought. When there is a drought, there is not enough ...rain ...soil ...sun.

© Houghton Mifflin Harcourt Publishing Company

13. When Grandfather told that silly story, he was in a jolly mood. *Jolly* means ...sad ...happy ...angry.

Say: Now go to the top of page 78 and find Sample B. In this part, you will find pictures to answer questions. I will read a story and then ask a question. You will find the picture that best answers the question. Put your finger on Sample B. Look at the pictures. Inez and Isabel are twins. Even though they look alike, they are very different. They like to do different things. They wear their hair the same way, but they always dress differently. Darken the circle for the picture that shows Inez and Isabel.

Say: The correct answer is the third picture. This picture shows two girls whose hair styles are the same but whose clothes are different.

Say: Now you will choose more pictures that best answer questions about stories that you hear. Do numbers 14 through 21 just as you did Sample B. Study the pictures, and listen carefully to the story and question. Then darken the circle under the correct answer.

Say:

14. Listen to the story. Jesse was playing in the park one afternoon. He saw a frisky squirrel jump from limb to limb in a tree. He also saw a beautiful butterfly land on a flower. As Jesse left the park to go home, he saw a small dinosaur smiling at him. Darken the circle for the picture that shows something from the story that could not happen.

15. Move to the next row. Listen to these directions for making strawberry ice cream:

    1. Mash two and a half cups of strawberries in a bowl.
    2. Mix one-fourth cup sugar and 8 tablespoons of vanilla together.
    3. Beat one cup whipping cream until it is thick.
    4. Combine all ingredients and place in the freezer.

    Look at the pictures. Which of these would you need to use when making the strawberry ice cream? Is it ...a toothbrush ...a tape measure ...or a measuring cup?

16. Move to the next row. Listen to the story. Sam and Rolando were walking in the woods one night. As they passed under a tree, Rolando felt something fall from the tree. What was it that fell from the tree? ...a spider web ...gum ...a leaf? Darken the circle for the correct answer.

17. Move to the next row. Listen to this story. Walter was getting ready to do an art project. He had his paper, paints, and a cup of water. "I only need one more thing," said Walter. What did Walter need to do his art project? Was it ...a crayon ...a paintbrush ...or a pencil?

18. Move to the next row. Listen to the story. Brooke loves her new musical instrument. She loves the sound it makes when she strums the strings. She likes to sing while she plays. What is Brooke's new instrument? ...a bugle ...a drum ...a guitar?

19. Move to the next row. Listen to this poem:

    I saw something move.

    It went under the rug.

    Finally, I found it.

    It was only a _____.

    Darken the circle for the picture that will rhyme with the poem.

20. Move to the next row. Listen to this story. Amy was excited. There were balloons, presents, and a cake for her. When the doorbell rang, she put on her hat. She had one just like it for each of her friends. They would have so much fun celebrating her birthday. Darken the circle for the picture that shows which hat Amy and her friends were wearing.

21. Move to the next row. Listen to the story. Forest Lane is an old country road. There is a covered bridge on Forest Lane that is wide enough for two cars to drive across at a time. Darken the circle for the picture that shows the bridge on Forest Lane.

Say: Now turn to the top of page 79 and find Sample C. In this part of the test, you will choose words and phrases that best answer questions about passages that you hear. I will read a passage and then ask a question. You will choose the best answer to the question. Listen as I read this poem. You will answer one question.

We see something in the sky,

Far away and very high.

Roaring by, it comes to land.

Not too far from where we stand.

What is the poem talking about? Is it ...a bird ...an airplane ...a rocket? Darken the circle for the correct answer.

Say: The correct answer is the second group of words, an airplane. The poem tells us that something that is roaring by is coming to land nearby. We can guess that the poem is talking about an airplane.

Say: Now you will choose more words and phrases that best answer questions about passages that you hear. Do numbers 22 through 32 just as you did Sample C. Listen carefully to the passage and question. Then darken the circle for the correct answer.

Say:

22. Listen carefully to this poem:

    The bird's nest had two small eggs.

    Today the eggs are gone somehow.

    Instead the nest has tiny legs

    And two hungry mouths to feed now.

    What happened to the eggs? Did they ...fall out of the nest ...get stolen by someone ...hatch into baby birds? Darken the circle for the correct answer.

23. Move to the next row. Listen to these directions for making a magic trick. You will answer one question.

    1. Fold a piece of white paper in half.

    2. On one side draw a goldfish. On the other side, draw a fishbowl.

    3. Tape a pencil inside the folded paper.

    4. Tape the open ends of the paper together.

    5. Roll the pencil quickly between your palms. You can watch the goldfish "jump" into the fishbowl!

    When you roll the pencil between your palms, the goldfish looks as if it is ...swimming in a river ...flipping around in the fishbowl ...swimming off the paper ...jumping into the fishbowl.

Say: Move to the next row. Listen to the story. You will answer two questions. Mr. Nelson stopped at a gas station to ask directions to the Pioneer Library. The attendant said, "Turn right at the next light on Pecan Street. Go down two blocks and take another right on Willow. You'll pass a school and a park. The library is on the right next door to a bank."

24. The library is next to ...a bank ...a school ...a river ...a store.

25. These directions are to a ...park ...shopping mall ...school ...library.

Say: Move to the next row. Listen carefully to this passage. You will answer three questions. There are many strange and interesting fish in the world. One of them is called a puffer fish. It lives in the ocean near coral reefs. Puffer fish have spines that stick out all over their bodies. They cannot swim very fast. A puffer fish can do something very unusual, which gives it its name. When it feels afraid, it puffs itself up like a balloon. Then the puffer fish looks bigger. It also looks brave. Then nothing will bother the funny puffer fish.

26. What is the best title for this passage? ..."The Balloon" ..."Ocean Creatures" ..."A Strange Kind of Fish" ... "Pretty Pets."

27. Where do puffer fish live? Is it ...in a pond ...in large lakes ...near coral reefs?

28. How does a puffer fish feel when it puffs itself up? Does it feel ...happy ...sad ...afraid?

Say: Move to the next row. Listen to this story. You will answer two questions. It was a warm summer day. Carlos was bathing his dog. First, he hooked up the water hose. Next, he got the special dog soap. He gently got the dog wet with water from the hose. Then, he used the soap to make lots of suds. Finally, he rinsed all the soap off the dog.

29. What is the best title for this story? ..."A Summer Day" ..."Taking Care of Pets" ..."Carlos Bathes the Dog."

30. What did Carlos do first to bathe the dog? Did he ...rinse the soap off ...hook up the water hose ...make lots of suds?

Say:

31. Move to the next row. Listen again to these directions for making a magic trick. You will answer one question.

    1. Fold a piece of white paper in half.

    2. On one side draw a goldfish. On the other side, draw a fishbowl.

    3. Tape a pencil inside the folded paper.

    4. Tape the open ends of the paper together.

    5. Roll the pencil quickly between your palms. You can watch the goldfish "jump" into the fishbowl!

    What should you tape inside the folded paper? Is it ...a ruler ...a pencil ...some stickers ...or a crayon?

32. Move to the last row. Listen to the story. Terri was very excited. Her cousin Amy was coming to visit. Amy was coming all the way from Florida. Terri and her mom would meet Amy at the bus station on Sunday afternoon. Darken the circle next to the words that tell where Terri and her mom would meet Amy. Is it ...at an airport ...at a bus station ...at home?

Sample A: extra, 1. first, 2. take part, 3. an answer,
4. blaze, 5. throw, 6. sure, 7. eat, 8. appreciate,
9. shine, 10. sunset, 11. rough, 12. rain, 13. happy,
Sample B: third picture, 14. first picture, 15. third
picture, 16. third picture, 17. second picture, 18. third
picture, 19. third picture, 20. second picture, 21. second
picture, Sample C: an airplane, 22. hatch into baby
birds, 23. jumping into the fishbowl, 24. a bank,
25. library, 26. "A Strange Kind of Fish", 27. near coral
reefs, 28. afraid, 29. "Carlos Bathes the Dog", 30. hook
up the water hose, 31. a pencil, 32. at a bus station

Unit 8

Pages 80–81

Say: You will practice choosing pictures, words, and phrases that answer questions about stories you hear. Move to the first row. This is Sample A. Listen to this poem:

Carla ate ice cream.

She made a big mess.

It dripped off the cone

and fell on her _____ .

Darken the circle for the picture that will rhyme with the poem.

Say: Now look at **Think It Through**. The correct answer is the first picture, the dress. In the poem, *dress* rhymes with *mess*.

Say: Now you will practice choosing more pictures that answer questions about stories you hear. Listen carefully. Then choose your answer from the pictures given for the story.

1. Place your finger under the next row. Look at the pictures of animals. I am going to tell you a story about Akio. Listen carefully to the story to find out which animal Akio petted. Akio liked to visit the pet store. The owner of the store let Akio help with the animals. Akio cleaned the birds' cages and then gave them water. He petted the rabbits. Then, he fed the many different fish. Darken the circle for the picture that shows which animal Akio petted.

2. Move to the next row. Listen to this story. Rudy the goldfish lives in a fishbowl. Once Rudy lived in a sparkling stream in the forest. Then he lived in a fish tank at the pet store. Darken the circle for the picture that shows where Rudy lives now.

3. Move to the last row. Listen to this story. Mr. Campos was making breakfast for his family. First, he cooked some bacon. Next, he cut up some oranges for juice. Finally, he scrambled some eggs and baked some muffins. Darken the circle for the picture that shows something Mr. Campos did when he was making breakfast.

Say: Now go to the top of page 81. In this part of the lesson you will practice choosing words and phrases that answer questions about stories you hear. When I read a passage, look at the words or phrases given in each row. Then, darken the circle for the word or phrase that goes with the passage. Place your finger under the first row. This is Sample B. Now listen carefully to this poem:

Mrs. Harper pulled out a book

and said it was time to bake.

She turned the pages to look

for a recipe to make a cake.

Was Mrs. Harper looking at ...a math book ...a cookbook ...or a reading book? Darken the circle next to the book Mrs. Harper was looking at.

Say: The correct answer is "a cookbook." Mrs. Harper was looking at a cookbook. Cookbooks have recipes that people can follow when they cook or bake.

Say: Now you will practice choosing more words or phrases that answer questions about stories you hear. Listen carefully to each story. Then, choose your answer from the words or phrases given for the story.

Say:

4. Listen carefully to this story. There will be two questions to answer about this story. Mr. Harris' second-grade class put on a play. Cara was a princess. Lori played an evil witch who put a spell on Cara. Tony was the prince who broke the spell by giving Cara a magic rose. "You have the best part in the play," Mr. Harris told Vinnie. "You get to be the dragon." Darken the circle next to the part Cara plays in the class play.

5. Move to the next row. What is the best title for this story? Is it ..."The Princess and the Witch" ..."The Class Play" ...or "Our Teacher, Mr. Harris"? Darken the circle next to the best title for this story.

6. Move to the next row. Listen to this poem:

I have a pet that's long and thin

and has scales for its skin.

When it crawls upon the ground,

it does not make a sound.

Is the poem talking about ...a fish ...a dog ...or a snake? Darken the circle next to the pet the poem talks about.

7. Move to the last row. Listen carefully to this story. Gloria helps her mother with the housework. Before going to school, Gloria makes her bed. After school, she does her homework. Finally, after dinner, she washes the dishes. Darken the circle next to the housework Gloria does first each day.

Answers: Pages 80–81

Sample A: picture of dress, **1.** picture of rabbit, **2.** second picture, **3.** third picture, **Sample B:** a cookbook, **4.** princess, **5.** "The Class Play", **6.** a snake, **7.** makes her bed

Pages 82–86

Say: You will practice finding words and sentences that answer questions about stories you hear. Now place your finger under the first row. This is Sample A. Look at the picture with the title "A Letter from Camp" while I read you a story about Max. Now listen carefully.

Say: Max is at a summer camp. He will write a letter to his family telling about his favorite camp activities. Look at the three boxes below "Letter to My Family." Now listen carefully. Max is deciding what to write in his letter. Which idea will Max not write about in his letter? Is it ...The food at school is good. ...I like to sail in the morning. ...or We have fun swimming when it is hot.? Darken the circle for the idea Max will not write about.

Say: Now look at **Think It Through**. The correct answer is "The food at school is good." Max wants to write about his camp activities in his letter. The pictures show Max swimming and sailing, so he will write about these activities.

Say: Now you will practice choosing more words and sentences that answer questions about passages you hear. Listen carefully to each passage. Then, choose your answer from the words and sentences given. Place your finger under the first row.

Say: Look at the poem with the title "Soccer Fun." Read it silently to yourself as I read it aloud.

Soccer Fun

Soccer is my favorite sport.

I like to run up and down the field.

Sometimes the ball I take away from the other team.

It is fun when I score a goal.

Say:

1. Look at the last sentence in "Soccer Fun" that says, "It is fun when I score a goal." Which sentence should be written next? Should it be ...I play soccer after school. ...My mother watches me play soccer. ...or Everyone cheers for me.? Darken the circle next to the sentence that should be written next.

Say:

2. Move to the next row. Look at the sentence in "Soccer Fun" that says, "Sometimes the ball I take away from the other team." Was this sentence written correctly? Should it be written ...The ball I take away sometimes from the other team. ...Sometimes I take the ball away from the other team. ...or is the sentence Correct the way it is? Darken the circle next to the way the sentence should be written.

Say: Now move to the next row. Look at the picture with the title "A Kick Out of Soccer" while I read you a story about Leila. Then, you will answer some questions about this story. Now listen carefully.

Say:

3. Leila's teacher asked the class to write a story about their favorite sport. Leila likes to play soccer. She decided to write about soccer. What should Leila do before she begins writing her story? Should she ...watch a soccer game ...draw a picture of herself playing soccer ...or make a list of reasons she likes soccer? Darken the circle next to the answer that tells what Leila should do before she begins writing her story.

4. Move to the next row. Write your answer to the following question. Why will Leila write a story about soccer?

Say: Go to the top of page 84. Now we will continue. Leila decided to write about her soccer team. Listen to what Leila wrote in her story. Read it silently to yourself as I read it aloud.

Say: The name of my team is the Panthers.

We practice two times each week.

To warm up, we <u>running</u> around the field.
  (1)

We also <u>kick</u> the ball to each other.
  (2)

My best friends are on my team.

We have so much fun together.

Say: Now place your finger under the first row.

5. Look at the underlined word with the number 2 under it. Did Leila use the right word? Should she write ...kicking ...kicked ...or is the word Correct the way it is? Darken the circle for the way Leila should write the underlined word.

6. Move to the last row. Look at the underlined word with the number 1 under it. Did Leila use the right word? Should she write ...ran ...run ...or is the word Correct the way it is? Darken the circle for the way Leila should write the underlined word.

Say: Go to the top of page 85. Place your finger under the first row. Look at the picture with the title "My Trip" while I read you a story about Dinah. Now listen carefully.

Say:

7. Dinah's family went on a trip. When Dinah got home, she made a book telling about all the things she had seen and done on her trip. She is not sure how to spell the word *visit*. She will look it up in the dictionary. Which word will probably be on the same page as *visit*? Is it ...*van* ...*train* ...or *water*? Darken the circle for the word that will probably be on the same page as *visit*.

8. Move to the next row. Look at the three boxes below "A Book About My Trip." Dinah is deciding what to write in her book. Which idea will Dinah not write about in her book? Is it ...Places we camped ...Places we visited ...or Places we wanted to visit? Darken the circle for the idea Dinah will not write about in her book.

Say: Now look at the Table of Contents. Listen carefully. Dinah put a Table of Contents at the front of her book. Read it silently to yourself as I read it aloud. Chapter 1 is called "The Beach" and begins on page 5. Chapter 2 is called "The Mountains" and begins on page 16. Chapter 3 is called "The Desert" and begins on page 27. Now place your finger under the row next to the Table of Contents.

Say:

9. Now listen carefully. What did Dinah write about on page 27? Is it ...rocks ...oceans ...or cactus? Darken the circle for what Dinah wrote about on page 27.

Say: Go to the top of page 86. Listen to what Dinah wrote about one part of her trip. Read it silently to yourself as I read it aloud.

Say: We saw a very tall cactus in the desert.

We asked a park ranger about it.

The park ranger's name was <u>Mr. elkhorn</u>.
  (1)

He said, "<u>A flower</u> will bloom on the cactus
  (2)

after it rains."

Say: Now place your finger under the first row.

10. Look at the underlined words with the number 1 under them. Did Dinah use correct capitalization to write these words? Write your answer for the way Dinah should write the underlined words.

11. Move to the next row. Look at the underlined words with the number 2 under them. Did Dinah use correct capitalization to write these words? Darken the circle for the way Dinah should write the underlined words.

Say: Now listen to Dinah's finished story. Read it silently to yourself as I read it aloud.

Travel Fun

My family went on a trip in June.

We slept in a tent every night.

My father cooked over a campfire.

We sang songs in school.

We went to many interesting places.

Say: Now place your finger under the next row.

12. Which sentence does not belong in the story? Is it ...My family went on a trip in June. ...My father cooked over a campfire. ... or We sang songs in school.? Darken the circle next to the sentence that does not belong in the story.

13. Move to the last row. Dinah wants to tell about a beach she visited. Which sentence would she probably write? Is it ...We had a picnic in the park. ...The huge waves crashed against the white sand. ...or I bought some colorful postcards.? Darken the circle next to the sentence Dinah will probably write about the beach.

Sample A: The food at school is good., **1.** Everyone cheers for me., **2.** Sometimes I take the ball away from the other team., **3.** make a list of reasons she likes soccer, **4.** Possible answer: to tell why she likes soccer, **5.** Correct the way it is, **6.** run, **7.** van, **8.** Places we wanted to visit, **9.** cactus, **10.** Mr. Elkhorn, **11.** Correct the way it is, **12.** We sang songs in school., **13.** The huge waves crashed against the white sand.

Page 87

Say: You will practice finding words that are not spelled correctly. Place your finger under the first row. This is Sample A. Now listen carefully to this sentence. The magical king granted the shoemaker three wishes. Darken the circle for the word that is not spelled correctly.

Say: Now look at **Think It Through**. The correct answer is the last underlined word: *wishs*. This word is not spelled correctly. The correct spelling of *wishes* is w-i-s-h-e-s.

Say: Now you will practice finding more words that are not spelled correctly. Do numbers 1 through 5 on your own.

Answers: Page 87

Sample A: wishs, **1.** slideing, **2.** carryed, **3.** char, **4.** storys, **5.** beging

Test: Pages 88–95

Say: Turn to the Test on page 88. In the first part of the test you will find pictures that answer questions about stories you hear. Place your finger under the first row. This is Sample A. Now listen carefully. Children should not play with matches. Izumi's little brother struck a match. He dropped the burning match onto a chair. Darken the circle for the picture of what probably happened next.

Say: The correct answer is the first picture. This picture shows something that probably happened next. The burning match could start a fire.

Say: Now you will find more pictures that answer questions about stories you hear. Place your finger under the next row.

Say:

1. Listen to this poem:

   I turned on the water

   and picked up the hose.

   I pulled it to the garden,

   so I could water the _____.

   Darken the circle for the picture that will rhyme with the poem.

2. Move to the next row. Mrs. York's class was learning about pollution and how to take good care of the Earth. She planned a number of projects for the students. On Monday, they picked up trash. On Wednesday, the students collected newspapers and empty soda cans. On Friday, they planted a tree in the school yard. Darken the circle for the picture that shows what the students did first.

3. Move to the next row. Matt built a snowman one winter. Chills the snowman was standing in the front yard. The weather started getting warmer. It was so sunny that Chills put on his sunglasses. The next day the weather was so warm that Chills melted into a puddle. Darken the circle for the picture that shows something from the story that could not happen.

4. Move to the last row. Ryan made muffins for the bake sale. He got out all of the ingredients. Then he got out the muffin pan. Darken the circle for the pan Ryan used.

Say: Go to the top of page 89. In the next part of the test you will choose words and phrases that answer questions about stories you hear. Place your finger under the first row. This is Sample B. Listen carefully to this story. Mel was baby-sitting. He played with the baby all evening. Soon, the baby started yawning. "It is time for you to go to bed," said Mel. He gave the baby a bath. Then, he fed the baby a bottle. Finally, Mel rocked the baby to sleep.

What is the best title for this story? Is it ..."Mel Plays with a Baby" ..."Bedtime for Baby" or ..."Mel's Baby-sitting Job"? Darken the circle next to the best title for this story.

Say: The correct answer is "Mel's Baby-sitting Job." The story is about Mel's baby-sitting job.

Say: Now you will find more words and phrases that answer questions about stories you hear.

5. Place your finger under the next row. This question is about the story you just heard. I will read it to you again. Mel was baby-sitting. He played with the baby all evening. Soon, the baby started yawning. "It is time for you to go to bed," said Mel. He gave the baby a bath. Then, he fed the baby a bottle. Finally, Mel rocked the baby to sleep. Darken the circle next to what Mel did first before getting the baby ready for bed.

Say:

6. Move to the next row. Listen to this story. Gina was very happy. She was going to visit her grandparents in Utah. She was going to ride in an

airplane all by herself. Gina's mother helped her pack. Write what Gina will travel in to visit her grandparents.

7. Move to the next row. Listen to this poem:

   I saw an animal in the wood

   Eating green leaves for food.

   It had a tail like a cotton ball

   And two ears standing tall.

   A sudden noise made it stop.

   Then off I saw it hop.

   Is the poem talking about a frog ...a rabbit ...or a donkey? Darken the circle next to the animal the poem talks about.

8. Move to the last row. Now listen carefully to this poem:

   The clock should wake me up at eight,

   but last night it fell to the floor.

   Today I got up much too late,

   since the clock can't ring anymore.

   Did the person writing the poem lose the clock ...forget to set the clock ...or break the clock? Darken the circle next to the phrase that tells what happened to the clock.

Say: Now go to the top of page 90. In the next part of the test you will find words and sentences that answer questions about stories you hear. Place your finger under the first row. This is Sample C. Look at the picture with the title "About Heather's Father" while I tell you a story about Heather. The school newspaper was looking for stories about people who worked in the town. Heather's father is a police officer. Heather decided to write a story about her father. Look at the three boxes below "Writing a Story." What should Heather do before writing her story? Should she ... Talk to her father ...Visit the newspaper office ...or Read a book about her town? Darken the circle for what Heather should do before writing her story.

Say: The correct answer is "Talk to her father." Heather should talk to her father to get information about what a police officer does.

Say:

9. Now place your finger under the next row. Heather should do something before she talks to her father. What should Heather do? Should she ...Ride in a police car ...Watch a movie about police officers ...or Make a list of questions to ask her father? Darken the circle next to what Heather should do before talking to her father.

Say: Now move to the next row. Listen to what Heather wrote in her story, "A Police Officer's Job." Read it silently to yourself as I read it aloud.

A Police Officer's Job

My father is a police officer.

He has an important job.

My bike has a flat tire.

He helps people who are hurt.

Sometimes he directs cars.

Say: Now move to the next row.

10. Which sentence does not belong in the story? Is it ...He has an important job. ...My bike has a flat tire. ...or He helps people who are hurt.? Write the sentence that does not belong in the story.

Say: Now go to the top of page 91. Look at the picture with the title "Going to the Moon" while I tell you a story about Randy. Randy's teacher asked the students to write a story about something they would like to do when they get older. Randy likes to read stories about traveling in space. He also likes to study the stars and the planets through his telescope. He wants to take a trip to the moon when he is older. He wants to learn more about the moon before he writes his story. So he got a book from the library. Look at the Table of Contents. Randy found this Table of Contents at the front of the library book. Read it to yourself as I read it aloud. Chapter 1 is called "How Far Away" and begins on page 2. Chapter 2 is called "What It's Made of" and begins on page 9. Chapter 3 is called "People on the Moon" and begins on page 25. Now place your finger under the row next to the Table of Contents.

Say:

11. When Randy looks at page 2, what will he read about? Will he read about ...The big holes on the moon ...The miles between the earth and moon ...or The first person who visited the moon? Darken the circle next to what Randy will read about on page 2.

12. Move to the last row. Now listen carefully. Which page would Randy turn to if he wanted to read about people who have visited the moon? Would he turn to page 2 ...9 ...or 25? Write the page Randy would turn to.

Say: Now go to the top of page 92. Listen to what Randy learned about the moon. Read it silently to yourself as I read it aloud.

The big holes is called craters.
(1)

I would <u>like</u> to go inside a crater.
(2)

It would be like walking inside a cave.

Say: Now place your finger under the first row.

13. Now listen carefully. Look at the word with the number 1 under it. Did Randy use the right word? Should he write ...are ...were ...or is the underlined word Correct the way it is? Write the way Randy should write the underlined word.

14. Move to the next row. Look at the word with the number 2 under it. Did Randy use the right word? Should he write ... liking ...likes ...or is the underlined word Correct the way it is? Darken the circle for the way Randy should write the underlined word.

Say: Move to the next row. Listen to what Randy wrote in his story. Read it silently to yourself as I read it aloud.

Seeing the Moon

The moon is very far away.

I would like to ride in a spaceship to get there.

A spacesuit I could wear to keep me safe.

I would like to see what is in the moon's big holes.

Say: Now move to the next row.

15. Which sentence would Randy probably write at the beginning of his story? Would it be ...When I get older, I want to visit the moon. ...The big holes are deep. ...or A spaceship moves very fast.? Darken the circle next to the sentence Randy will probably write at the beginning of his story.

16. Move to the last row. Look at the sentence that says, "A spacesuit I could wear to keep me safe." Did Randy write the sentence correctly? Should he write ...A spacesuit to keep me safe I could wear. ...I could wear a spacesuit to keep me safe. ...or is the sentence Correct the way it is? Darken the circle next to the way Randy should write the sentence.

Say: Now go to the top of page 93. Look at the picture under the title "Visiting Aunt Donna" while I tell you a story about Shakia. Now listen carefully. Shakia is going to visit her Aunt Donna. Aunt Donna lives on a farm. Shakia decided to write a letter to let her aunt know when she would arrive. Listen to the first part of Shakia's letter. Read it silently to yourself as I read it aloud.

Dear Aunt Donna,

Thank you for inviting me to visit.

The farm this summer.

<u>May I stay for two weeks</u>

I want to learn how to take care of animals.

Say: Now move to the next row.

17. Which group of words does not make a complete sentence? Is it ... Thank you for inviting me to visit. ...The farm this summer. ...or I want to learn how to take care of animals.? Write the group of words that does not make a complete sentence.

18. Move to the next row. Which sentence should Shakia write next? Should she write ...I want to milk and feed the cows and chickens. ... The cows I want to milk and the chickens I want to feed. ...or I want to milk the cow and feed the chickens.? Darken the circle next to the sentence Shakia should write next.

19. Move to the last row. Look at the underlined sentence in Shakia's letter. Which punctuation mark should Shakia place at the end of the underlined sentence? Darken the circle for the punctuation mark Shakia should write at the end of the underlined sentence.

Say: Now go to the top of page 94. Listen to what Shakia wrote later in her letter. Read it to yourself as I read it aloud.

I am leaving this <u>tuesday</u>.
(1)

<u>Will you pick me up at the bus station</u>
(2)

I can't wait to see you.

Love,

Shakia

Say: Now move to the next row.

20. Look at the underlined sentence with the number 2 under it. Which punctuation mark should Shakia place at the end of the sentence? Write the punctuation mark Shakia should write at the end of the underlined sentence.

21. Move to the last row. Look at the underlined word with the number 1 under it. Did Shakia write the word with the correct capitalization? Darken the circle for the way Shakia should write the underlined word.

Say: Now go to the top of page 95. In the last part of the test you will find words that are not spelled correctly. Place your finger under the first row. This is Sample D. Look at the sentence. Read it to

© Houghton Mifflin Harcourt Publishing Company

yourself as I read it aloud.

My sister is arriveing tomorrow from Canada.

Say: Darken the circle for the underlined word that is not spelled correctly.

Say: The correct answer is the second underlined word. *Arriveing* is correctly spelled a-r-r-i-v-i-n-g.

Say: Now you will find more words that are not spelled correctly. Place your finger under the next row. Do numbers 22 through 29 on your own.

Answers: Pages 88–95

Sample A: first picture, **1.** third picture, **2.** second picture, **3.** first picture, **4.** first picture,

Unit 9

Practice Test 1: Pages 96–102

(Allow 35 minutes for this test.)

Say: In this test you will use your reading skills to answer questions about stories that you read. Look at Sample A. We will work the sample together. Read the story and the question in Sample A. How does Jim get to school? Then, darken the circle beside the correct answer.

Say: The correct answer is "He rides a bus." The last sentence of the story tells us that Jim rides a bus to school because he lives too far to walk.

Say: Now you will answer more questions about stories that you read. Put your finger on number 1. Do numbers 1 through 26 just as you did Sample A. Read each selection carefully. Then, read the questions. Darken the circle beside the correct answer. You have 35 minutes to complete the test. You may now begin.

Unit 10

Practice Test 2, part 1: Pages 103–104

(Allow 20 minutes for this test.)

Say: In this part of the test you will use your word study skills to answer questions. This part of the test is divided into four sections. For each section there is a sample exercise. We will work each sample together. In the first section of the test, you will find compound words. Put your finger under Sample A. Look at the words *neighbor*, *money*, and *starfish*. Which of the these words is made up of two words? Darken the circle under the compound word.

Say: The correct answer is "starfish," because *starfish* is a compound word made up of the words *star* and *fish*.

Sample B: "Mel's Baby-sitting Job", **5.** gave the baby a bath, **6.** an airplane, **7.** a rabbit, **8.** break the clock, **Sample C:** Talk to her father, **9.** Make a list of questions to ask her father, **10.** My bike has a flat tire., **11.** The miles between the earth and moon, **12.** 25, **13.** are, **14.** Correct the way it is, **15.** When I get older, I want to visit the moon., **16.** I could wear a spacesuit to keep me safe., **17.** The farm this summer., **18.** I want to milk the cows and feed the chickens., **19.** weeks?, **20.** ?, **21.** Tuesday, **Sample D:** arriveing, **22.** Wher, **23.** tern, **24.** hoping, **25.** frendly, **26.** Watr, **27.** butterflys, **28.** pushs, **29.** boxs

Answers: Pages 96–102

Sample A: He rides a bus., **1.** Curtis did a good job., **2.** a car, **3.** in the morning., **4.** rake leaves., **5.** Tia and Clyde splashed in the water., **6.** "A Girl and Her Donkey", **7.** in the mountains, **8.** The path was dangerous., **9.** a year of growth., **10.** count the rings, **11.** It is young., **12.** read a book about the life of a tree, **13.** add the banana., **14.** sandwich., **15.** two, **16.** something you may or may not do., **17.** the man who works at the lighthouse., **18.** so that sailors at sea can find land, **19.** She is excited about the visit and wants to come back., **20.** jobs, **21.** tell about a special lighthouse., **22.** "A Visit to a Lighthouse", **23.** "Why Ducks Like Water", **24.** Big feet help them push the water., **25.** climb, **26.** to eat it

Say: Now you will find more compound words. Put your finger under the group of words in number 1. Do numbers 1 through 6 just as you did Sample A. Darken the circle under the correct answer. You have about 10 minutes to complete this part of the test. You may now begin.

Say: Now go to Sample B at the top of the second column. In the next section of the test, you will match printed words with words that you hear. Put your finger under Sample B. Look at the words *quicker* ...*quickest* ...and *quickly*. These words are similar, but they do not have the same ending. Listen carefully as I say a word and read it in a sentence. Darken the circle under the word *quickly*. Frank ran *quickly*. *Quickly*.

Say: The correct answer is the last word, "quickly." Although *quick* is a part of each word, *quickly* is the word that you heard.

Say: Now you will match more printed words with words that you hear. Put your finger under the group of words in number 7. You will do numbers 7 through 12 just as you did Sample B. Listen carefully to the word and the sentence. Then, darken the circle under the correct answer.

Say:

7. Darken the circle under the word *worker*. Russell is a hard *worker*. *Worker*.

8. Move to the next group of words. Darken the circle under the word *runner*. She was a fast *runner*. *Runner*.

9. Move to the next group of words. Darken the circle under the word *filled*. Jess *filled* the glasses with ice. *Filled*.

10. Move to the next group of words. Darken the circle under the word *added*. The clerk *added* up our bill. *Added*.

11. Move to the next group of words. Darken the circle under the word *rains*. If it *rains*, the game will be canceled. *Rains*.

12. Move to the last group of words. Darken the circle under the word *softest*. The rabbit had the *softest* fur. *Softest*.

Say: Now go to the top of page 104 and find Sample C. In this part of the test, you will find contractions. Look at the words *who'd ...who'll ...*and *who's*. Each of these words is a shortened form, or a contraction, of two other words. I will say two words and use them in a sentence. You will find the contraction that has the same meaning as the two words I say. Listen carefully. Darken the circle under the word that means *who will*. *Who will* help Petra? *Who will*.

Say: The correct answer is "who'll," because *who'll* is the contraction of *who will*.

Say: Now you will find more contractions. Put your finger under the group of words in number 13. You will do numbers 13 through 18 just as you did Sample C. Listen carefully to the two words and the sentence I say. Then, darken the circle under the correct answer.

Say:

13. Darken the circle under the word that means *it will*. *It will* be dark soon. *It will*.

14. Move to the next group of words. Darken the circle under the word that means *I have*. *I have*

always wanted to visit Florida. *I have*.

15. Move to the next group of words. Darken the circle under the word that means *does not*. Heather *does not* want to go. *Does not*.

16. Move to the next group of words. Darken the circle under the word that means *are not*. The birds *are not* in their nest. *Are not*.

17. Move to the next group of words. Darken the circle under the word that means *cannot*. We *cannot* give up. *Cannot*.

18. Move to the last group of words. Darken the circle under the word that means *could have*. I *could have* bought something, but I saved my money. *Could have*.

Say: Now find Sample D at the top of the second column. In the last section, you will match printed words that have the same sound or sounds. Put your finger under Sample D. Look at the word *space* and the three answer choices. Notice that the *c* in *space* is underlined. Decide how the underlined part of the word sounds. Then, darken the circle under the word that has the same sound as the underlined *c* in *space*.

Say: The correct answer is "center," because the *c* in *center* has the same sound as the underlined *c* in *space*.

Say: Now you will match more words that have the same sound or sounds. Put your finger under the group of words in number 19. You will do numbers 19 through 24 just as you did Sample D. Look at the first word in each row and say it silently to yourself. Then, darken the circle under the correct answer. You have about 10 minutes to complete the test.

Answers: Pages 103–104

Sample A: starfish, **1.** ladybug, **2.** inside, **3.** something, **4.** myself, **5.** cupcake, **6.** suitcase, **Sample B:** quickly, **7.** worker, **8.** runner, **9.** filled, **10.** added, **11.** rains, **12.** softest, **Sample C:** who'll, **13.** it'll, **14.** I've, **15.** doesn't, **16.** aren't, **17.** can't, **18.** could've, **Sample D:** center, **19.** knee, **20.** shy, **21.** jaw, **22.** road, **23.** enjoy, **24.** locking

Practice Test 2, part 2: Pages 105–107

(Allow 30 minutes for this test.)

Say: In this part of the test you will use your reading vocabulary skills to answer questions. This part of the test is divided into three sections. For each section there is a sample exercise. We will work each sample together. Put your finger under Sample A. In this section of the test, you will find words that have the same or almost the same meaning as underlined words. Read the sentence and the four answer choices: "Something that is tiny is — metal ...broken ...small ...rich." Darken the circle beside the word that has the same or almost the same meaning as the underlined word, *tiny*.

Say: The correct answer is "small," because *tiny* has the same meaning as *small*.

Say: Now you will find the meaning of more words. Do numbers 1 through 9 just as you did Sample A. Darken the circle beside the correct answer. You have 10 minutes to complete this section. You may now begin.

Say: Now go to the top of page 106. In this part of the test, you will match words that have more than one meaning. Look at Sample B. Read the sentence in the box and the four answer choices: "We ate lunch out on the deck." In which sentence does the word *deck* mean the same as it does in the sentence in the box? ...Let's deck the room with streamers. ...I'll get a deck of cards. ...Jake built a new wood deck. ...I'm on the top deck of the boat. Darken the circle for the sentence that uses the word *deck* in the same way as the sentence in the box.

Say: The correct answer is the third sentence, "Jake built a new wood deck." In this sentence and in the sentence in the box, the word *deck* means "a wooden platform."

Say: Now you will match more words that have more than one meaning. Do numbers 10 through 13 just

as you did Sample B. Darken the circle beside the correct answer, or write in your answer. You have 10 minutes to complete this section. You may now begin.

Say: Now go to the top of page 107. Find Sample C. In the last section, you will use clue words to help you figure out the meaning of the underlined word. Read the sentence and the four answer choices: "Uncle Luis repaired the broken machine. *Repaired* means — fixed ...sold ...lost ...washed." Darken the circle beside the word that has the same meaning as the underlined word, *repaired*.

Say: The correct answer is "fixed," because *fixed* has almost the same meaning as *repaired*.

Say: Now you will use clue words to find the meaning of more words. Do numbers 14 through 20 just as you did Sample C. Darken the circle beside each correct answer. You have 10 minutes to complete this section. You may now begin.

Answers: Pages 105–107
Sample A: small, **1.** nearer, **2.** talk softly, **3.** look for, **4.** moving, **5.** rug, **6.** silly, **7.** train, **8.** laugh, **9.** plate, **Sample B:** Jake built a new wood deck., **10.** I will bat the ball to the fence., **11.** The small boat began to float on the lake., **12.** Answers will vary. Possible answer: We saw her dip underwater., **13.** Flowers grow along the river bank., **Sample C:** fixed, **14.** well-known, **15.** copied, **16.** move, **17.** hurt, **18.** Possible answer: write, **19.** strong, **20.** hide

Unit 11

Practice Test 3: Pages 108–113

(Allow 50 minutes for this test. Distribute scratch paper, an inch ruler, and a centimeter ruler to the child. These things may be used to solve some problems.)

Say: In this test you will choose pictures and numbers that answer math problems you hear. Place your finger under the first row. This is Sample A. Now listen carefully. Darken the circle under the correct way to write 300 plus 10.

Say: The correct answer is the second answer choice. This shows the number 310.

Say: Now you will choose more pictures and numbers that answer math problems you hear. You will do problems 1 through 29 just as you did Sample A. Place your finger under the row for number 1. Listen carefully.

Say:

1. Look at the picture of the bucket and paintbrushes. Darken the circle under the brush that is fifth from the bucket.

2. Move to the row for number 2. Darken the circle under the number that means *two hundreds, three tens, and four ones*.

3. Move to the row for number 3. Darken the circle under the number that is between 43 and 68.

4. Move to the row for number 4. Darken the circle under the number *one hundred seventy-three*.

5. Move to the last row for number 5. Write the number that tells how many marbles are shown in the picture.

Say: Go to the top of page 109. Place your finger under the row for number 6.

6. Darken the circle under another way to write *four times three.*

7. Move to the row for number 7. Look at the numbers. Write the number that is 100 more than 821.

8. Move to the row for number 8. Meiko is at summer camp. She sleeps in a tent that has an even number written on it. Darken the circle under Meiko's tent.

9. Move to the row for number 9. Darken the circle under the number that goes in the box to make the number sentence correct.

10. Move to the last row for number 10. The number sentence *ten minus nine* describes this picture. Darken the circle under another number sentence that describes this same picture.

Say: Go to the top of page 110. Place your finger under the row for number 11.

Say:

11. Darken the circle under the picture that shows three fourths of the flags shaded.

12. Move to the row for number 12. Look at the numbers in the boxes. These numbers make a pattern. Darken the circle under the number that is missing in the pattern.

13. Move to the row for number 13. Look at the four shapes. Darken the circle under the shape that is not divided into fourths.

14. Move to the row for number 14. Look at the stamps. Listen carefully. Felipe is counting his stamps to see how many stamps he has. He counts 73, 74, 75. Darken the circle under the stamp that would be 83.

15. Move to the last row for number 15. Darken the circle under the fraction that tells what part of the circle is shaded.

Say: Go to the top of page 111. Look at the chart with the title "Students Playing Musical Instruments." The chart shows the instruments and the number of students that play them in Mrs. Irwin's class. You will use this chart to answer numbers 16 and 17.

Say:

16. Look at the chart. Darken the circle under the number that tells how many students play guitar.

17. Move to the row for number 17. Look at the chart. Write the number that tells how many more students play drums than trumpets.

18. Move to the row for number 18. Look at the card at the beginning of the row. Carly cut a shape from this card. Darken the circle under the picture that shows the shape Carly cut from the card.

19. Move to the last row on the page for number 19. Look at the tally chart. Lou, Laurie, Alex, and Patti played soccer. The tally chart shows how many points each person scored. Write the name of the person who scored the fewest number of points.

Say: Go to the top of page 112. Place your finger under the row for number 20.

Say:

20. Darken the circle under the shortest pencil.

21. Move to the row for number 21. Look at the figure at the beginning of the row. Darken the circle under the figure that is exactly the same as the one at the beginning of the row.

22. Move to the row for number 22. Tina puts these shape blocks into a box. She will pull one shape out of the box. Darken the circle under the shape that Tina will most likely pull out of the box.

23. Move to the row for number 23. Darken the circle under the time shown on the clock.

24. Move to the last row for number 24. Darken the circle under the shape whose parts will not match exactly when it is folded on the dotted line.

Say: Go to the top of page 113. Place your finger under the row for number 25.

Say:

25. Use your centimeter ruler to help you answer this math problem. Darken the circle under the number that tells how many centimeters long the pen is.

26. Move to the row for number 26. Jesse has a quarter and a penny. Darken the circle under the number that tells the value of the coins.

27. Look at the clocks in number 27. The clocks show the time that Vincente started and completed his homework. How long did it take Vincente to do his homework? Write your answer.

28. Move to the row for number 28. Joy has the coins shown here. She wants to buy the ring shown in the picture. Darken the circle under the number that tells the money Joy will have left.

29. Move to the last row for number 29. Look at the baseball bat and the three baseballs below the baseball bat. You will use the baseballs to measure the length of the baseball bat. Darken the circle under the number that tells how many baseballs long the bat is.

Sample A: 310, **1.** The second circle should be darkened., **2.** 234, **3.** 55, **4.** 173, **5.** 30, **6.** 3 + 3 + 3 + 3, **7.** 921, **8.** tent number 12, **9.** 0, **10.** 9 + 1 = 10, **11.** first picture, **12.** 30, **13.** second picture **14.** The first circle should be darkened., **15.** $\frac{1}{5}$, **16.** 8, **17.** 2,

18. The third circle should be darkened., **19.** Alex, **20.** second picture, **21.** The third circle should be darkened., **22.** The first circle should be darkened., **23.** 2:15, **24.** The third circle should be darkened., **25.** 7, **26.** 26 cents, **27.** 1 hour, **28.** 12 cents, **29.** 9

Unit 12

Practice Test 4: Pages 114–116

(Allow 25 minutes for this test.)

Say: In this test you will use your listening skills to answer questions. This test is divided into three parts. For each part there is a sample exercise. We will work each sample together. Put your finger under the first row. This is Sample A. In this part of the test, you will find the words that best complete sentences. I will read a sentence and three words. You will find the word that best completes the sentence. Look at the three words in Sample A. Listen carefully. LaKrisha is searching for her lost book. *To search* is to — talk about ...think about ... look for. Darken the circle for the correct answer.

Say: The correct answer is the last choice, "look for," because *to search* means *to look for*.

Say: Now you will find more words that best complete sentences. Do numbers 1 through 13 just as you did Sample A. Listen carefully to the sentence and the three answer choices. Then darken the circle beside the correct answer.

Say:

1. The kitten pounced every time someone moved. *To pounce* means to — growl ...jump ...bite.

2. Move to the next row. The piano recital is in one month. A month is — four weeks ... several hours ...seven days.

3. Move to the next row. My parents like to stroll in the park. *To stroll* means to — run ...walk ...play.

4. Move to the next row. That tree limb is blocking the window. A limb is a — branch ...board ...ladder.

5. Move to the next row. Anita has always wanted to be an author. An author is a — writer ...dancer ... baker.

6. Move to the next row. Tonight we are having guests to dinner. A guest is — an answer ...a visitor ...a new dish.

7. Move to the next row. The principal motioned to the boys in the hall. *To motion* means to — say hello ...tell a story ...give a signal.

8. Move to the next row. Those flowers may wilt indoors. *To wilt* means to — droop ...grow ...open.

9. Move to the next row. Lucia packed her trunk for camp. A trunk is most like a — purse ...suitcase ...billfold.

10. Move to the next row. Which nation has the most people? A nation is a — country ...city ...state.

11. Move to the next row. The traffic came to an abrupt stop. *Abrupt* means about the same as — slow ...quick ...careful.

12. Move to the next row. The drums gave the music a steady beat. *Steady* means — even ...bigger ...angry.

13. Move to the last row. We are studying animals that live in marshes. A marsh is about the same as — a forest ...a swamp ...a jungle.

Say: Now go to the top of page 115 and find Sample B. In this part of the test, you will choose pictures that answer questions. Study the pictures. I will read a story and then ask a question. You will find the picture that best answers the question. Listen carefully. Scott and his family went to an orchard to get fresh fruit. Scott and his sister picked the fruit. When they got home, Scott's mother baked pies with the fruit they had picked. What could Scott have picked at the orchard? Was it ...a carrot ...corn ...or an apple?

Say: The correct answer is the third picture. The third picture shows an apple, which Scott could have picked at the orchard.

Say: Now you will choose more pictures that best answer questions. Do numbers 14 through 21 just as you did Sample B. Listen carefully to the passage and the question. Then, darken the circle under the picture for each correct answer.

Say:

14. Chad and Celeste built a sand castle in the sandbox in their yard. When they went into the house to eat lunch, it started raining very hard. When the rainstorm ended, the children went outside again. Darken the circle for the picture that shows what probably happened to the sand castle.

15. Move to the next row. The building downtown was tall. It had lots of windows and even had some plants on the roof. Darken the circle for the picture that shows how the building probably looked.

16. Move to the next row. Olga is writing a puppet play to show her friends. She wants to write many jokes in the play so her friends will laugh. Why is Olga writing the play? Is it ...to show to her friends ...to make a video at a television station ...or to pass the time while she is sick at home? Darken the circle under the picture that shows why Olga is writing the puppet play.

17. Move to the next row. Every morning before Kevin goes to school, he does three things. First, he eats breakfast. Then, he empties the trash. After that, he feeds the dog. What does Kevin do first? He ...feeds the dog ...empties the trash ...eats breakfast.

18. Move to top of the right column. Listen to this poem:

    Tim got some paper and scissors and glue.

    He got markers and paints and crayons, too.

    He set to work and worked very hard.

    Making for Mom a beautiful _____.

    Darken the circle for the picture that will rhyme with the poem.

19. Move to the next row. Kadijah wants to earn her nature badge in her scout troop. Her dad is taking her camping next weekend in a national park. When she returns from her camping trip, Kadijah must write a story about what she saw and did to earn her nature badge. Where would Kadijah find information about the kinds of animals that live in the national park? Darken the circle under the picture that shows where Kadijah would find information about the park animals.

20. Move to the next row. Who would Kadijah talk to to get more information about the national park — a park ranger ...her dad ...or a clerk at the camping store? Darken the circle under the picture that shows who Kadijah should talk to about the park.

21. Is Kadijah writing a story ...to report to her scout troop ...to earn her nature badge ...or to thank her dad for taking her camping? Darken the circle under the picture that shows why Kadijah is writing a story.

Say: Now go to the top of page 116 and find Sample C. In this part of the test, you will choose the words that best answer questions. I will read a passage and then ask a question. You will choose the best answer to the question. Listen carefully to this poem:

As Jason ran to catch the ball,

He did not see the stump.

He yelled as he began to fall.

His head now has a bump!

Did Jason fall because he tripped over ...a ball ...a stump ...or a friend? Darken the circle next to the word that tells what Jason tripped over.

Say: The correct answer is the second choice, a stump. Jason tripped over a stump while trying to catch the ball.

Say: Now you will choose more words that best answer questions. Do numbers 22 through 31 just as you did Sample C. Listen carefully to the passage and the question. Then darken the circle beside each correct answer.

Say: Listen to these rules. You will answer two questions. All visitors to Big Sandy Beach must follow these rules:

    1. No littering — trash containers are provided.

    2. No glass bottles or containers allowed on the beach.

    3. No dogs allowed.

    4. No children under ten allowed without an adult.

Say:

22. What is not allowed on Big Sandy Beach? Is it ...children over ten ...dogs ...or plastic containers?

23. Move to the next row. What should visitors do with litter? ...carry it home ...bury it in the sand ...put it in the trash containers.

Say: Move to the next row. Listen as I read this story. You will answer two questions. Juan helped his grandmother prepare dinner. First, he made a salad. Next, he made a pitcher of lemonade. Finally, he set the table.

24. What did Juan do second to help prepare dinner? Did he ...make a salad ...set the table ...make lemonade?

25. Was Juan helping his ...mother ...father ...grandmother?

Say: Listen to the passage. You will answer three questions. An eagle is a big bird, so it must have a big home. An eagle's home is called an eyrie. An eagle builds its eyrie with large sticks. It uses grass and leaves to make a soft lining for it. An eagle can use the same eyrie for many years. It adds on to and repairs its homes, just like some people do.

Say:

26. You can tell from the paragraph that an eyrie is a kind of ...nest ...bird ...statue ...birdbath.

© Houghton Mifflin Harcourt Publishing Company

27. Move to the next row. An eagle uses all of the following to build an eyrie except ...large sticks ...grass ...leaves ...small rocks.

28. Place your finger under the next row. An eagle uses the same eyrie for ...only one year ...two years ...three years ...many years.

Say: Move to the next row. Listen to this story. You will answer three questions. Ryan couldn't wait to tell his dad about his day. He and Grandma had gone to a very special place — the library. First, Ryan and Grandma watched a puppet show. It was a funny story, and everyone laughed a lot. Then, Ryan and Grandma found some books. There were many to choose from. Ryan found a few books and sat at a small table to look at them. Grandma went to another area and found some gardening books. When she came back, the librarian came over to talk to them. She showed Ryan many different things the library had: all kinds of books to use or check out, magazines to look at, videos and records to check out, even oil paintings for loan. Ryan was amazed. Before they left, the librarian issued Ryan his very own library card. All Ryan had to do was promise to take very good care of the things he

checked out and return them when they were due back.

29. Does Ryan think the library is a ...boring place ...scary place ...lonely place ...wonderful place?

30. Move to the next row. The librarian told Ryan about all of the following except ...magazines ...videos ...baseball cards ...different kinds of books.

31. Move to the last row on the page. Ryan got a library card by ...paying money ...doing work ...making a promise ...mailing in a coupon.

Answers: Pages 114–116

Sample A: look for, **1.** jump, **2.** four weeks, **3.** walk, **4.** branch, **5.** writer, **6.** a visitor, **7.** give a signal, **8.** droop, **9.** suitcase, **10.** country, **11.** quick, **12.** even, **13.** a swamp, **Sample B:** picture of apple, **14.** third picture, **15.** third picture, **16.** first picture, **17.** third picture, **18.** second picture, **19.** third picture, **20.** first picture, **21.** second picture, **Sample C:** a stump, **22.** dogs, **23.** put it in the trash containers, **24.** make lemonade, **25.** grandmother, **26.** nest, **27.** small rocks, **28.** many years, **29.** wonderful place, **30.** baseball cards, **31.** making a promise

Unit 13

Practice Test 5: Pages 117–127

(Allow 35 minutes for this test.)

Say: In the first part of the test you will find pictures that answer questions about stories you hear. Place your finger under the first row. This is Sample A. Listen to this poem:

Ben put a worm onto the hook

and made a special wish.

He wanted more than anything

to catch a great big _____.

Darken the circle for the picture that will rhyme with the poem.

Say: The correct answer is the second picture, which shows a fish. *Fish* rhymes with *wish*.

Say: Now you will find more pictures that answer questions about stories you hear. Place your finger under the next row.

1. In science, the class learned that heat can make things melt. We made a list of things that melt. Darken the circle for the picture that shows something that does not melt.

2. Move to the next row. Dana visited her grandparents' farm. It was harvest time, and she helped pick the vegetables. Dana sat in the kitchen and pulled off the husks while Grandma made dinner. Darken the circle for the picture that shows the vegetable with the husk.

3. Move to the next row. We have a pet duck named Quackers. Sometimes he likes to swim in the lake with us. Quackers enjoys eating the water plants that grow near the lake. At other times, while we splash and play in the lake, Quackers likes to ride his bike. Darken the circle for the picture that shows something from the story that could not happen.

4. Move to the last row. Every Saturday Andrew has three jobs that he does before he plays with his friends. First, he washes the breakfast dishes. Next, he waters his mom's plants. Then, he helps his dad rake leaves. Darken the circle for the picture that shows what job Andrew does first.

Say: Now go to the top of page 118. In the next part of the test you will choose words and phrases that answer questions about stories you hear. Place your finger under the first row. This is Sample B.

Juan helped his grandmother prepare dinner. First, he made a salad. Next, he made a pitcher of lemonade. Finally, he set the table. Darken the circle next to what Juan did second to help his grandmother prepare dinner.

Say: The correct answer is "made a pitcher of lemonade." The second thing Juan did was make a pitcher of lemonade.

Say: Now you will find more phrases and sentences that answer questions about stories you hear. Place your finger under the next row.

5. Now listen carefully to this poem:

    We know a bird named Jake,

    A heron, proud and tall,

    He stands on one leg by the lake,

    from summer into fall.

    Is Jake a fish ...a heron ...or a boy? Darken the circle next to the word that tells what Jake is.

6. Move to the next row. Listen to this story. You will answer two questions about this story. It was Mother's Day. Janey wanted to surprise her mother. She washed the clothes and hung them outside to dry. When they were dry, Janey folded the towels and sheets. Then she ironed the shirts. When Mother came home, Janey said, "Happy Mother's Day! I wanted to surprise you." Mother gave Janey a big hug. What is the best title for this story? Is it "Janey's Job," "A Mother's Day Surprise," or "Washing Clothes"? Darken the circle next to the best title for this story.

7. Move to the next row. Write what Janey did first to surprise her mother.

8. Move to the last row. Listen to this poem:

    Oscar made a lot of noise

    with one of his newest toys.

    A wooden stick was in each hand.

    He played he was in the band.

    He beat the toy so hard and loud

    and marched around the ground.

    Is the poem talking about a bugle ...a drum ...or a bell? Darken the circle next to the toy the poem is talking about.

Say: Now go to the top of page 119. In the next part of the test you will find words and sentences that answer questions about stories you hear. Look at Sample C. Listen while I tell you a story about Ingrid. Ingrid was having a birthday party. She was going to write her own party invitations. This is

what she first wrote. Read it silently to yourself as I read it aloud.

I <u>hope</u> to see you at my party.

Please let me know if you can come.

> Your friend,
>
> Ingrid

Look at the underlined word. Did Ingrid use the correct word? Should she write ...hoped ...hoping ...or is the underlined word Correct the way it is? Darken the circle for the way Ingrid should write the underlined word.

Say: The correct answer is "Correct the way it is." Ingrid used the correct word in the sentence.

Say: Now place your finger under the next row. This is Sample D. Ingrid realized she had to let everyone know when her party was. Listen to what Ingrid added to her invitations. Read it silently to yourself as I read it aloud.

I am having a birthday party.

On Friday at two o'clock.

We will play games at my house.

Now listen carefully. Which group of words does not make a complete sentence? Is it ...I am having a birthday party. ...On Friday at two o'clock. ...or We will play games at my house.? Darken the circle next to the group of words that does not make a complete sentence.

Say: The correct answer is "On Friday at two o'clock." This answer is not a complete sentence.

Say: Move to the next row. This is Sample E. Look at the picture with the title "My Birthday Party." Now listen carefully. Look at the three boxes below the box that reads "Writing Invitations." What did Ingrid not write about in her invitations? Was it ...The people she will invite ...The time of the party ...or Where the party will be? Darken the circle for what Ingrid did not write about in her invitation.

Say: The correct answer is "The people she will invite." Ingrid did not write about the people she will invite to her party in the invitations.

Say: Now go to the top of page 120. Sal's class was studying food and nutrition. The teacher asked the students to keep a diary for one week telling what kinds of foods they ate. She wanted them to find out if they ate healthy meals and snacks.

Now listen to what Sal wrote in the first part of his diary, under the title "A Big Breakfast." Read it silently to yourself as I read it aloud.

A Big Breakfast

I was hungry when I woke up.

I poured a glass of milk for everyone.

A glass of orange juice I also drank.

Father made banana muffins.

Say:

9. Now place your finger under the first row. Look at the last sentence Sal wrote. It says, "Father made banana muffins." Which sentence will Sal probably write next? Will it be ...I didn't drink all of my milk. ...I will eat an apple for a snack. ...or The muffins were so good that I ate two.? Write in the sentence Sal will probably write next.

10. Move to the next row. Look at the sentence that says, "A glass of orange juice I also drank." Did Sal write the sentence correctly? Should he write ...I also drank a glass of orange juice. ...I drank a glass also of orange juice. ...or is the sentence Correct the way it is? Darken the circle next to the way Sal should write the sentence.

Say: Now look at the picture with the title "Healthy Food" and listen carefully.

11. Move to the next row. What did Sal do before he wrote in his diary? Did he ...ask his mother what his family will eat for dinner ...make a list of healthy foods ...or think about the food he ate during the day? Darken the circle next to what Sal did before writing in his diary.

12. Move to the last row. Why is Sal writing in a diary? Is it ...to find out if he eats good food ...to write a food menu ...or to tell about his favorite foods? Darken the circle next to why Sal is writing in a diary.

Say: Now go to the top of page 121. Look at what Sal wrote later in his diary. Read it silently to yourself as I read it aloud.

I <u>gone</u> to a friend's house for dinner.
$\overline{(1)}$

We ate hot dogs.

Hot dogs <u>are</u> my favorite food.
$\overline{(2)}$

We had salad and peas, too.

Of course, I drank another glass of milk.

Say:

13. Now place your finger under the first row. Look at the word with the number 2 under it. Did Sal use the correct word? Should he write ...is ...was ...or is the underlined word Correct the way it is?

Darken the circle for the way Sal should write the underlined word.

14. Move to the last row. Look at the word with the number 1 under it. Did Sal use the correct word? Should he write ...is going ...went ...or is the underlined word Correct the way it is? Write the word Sal should use instead of the underlined word.

Say: Now go to the top of page 122. Look at the picture with the title "Talking to Grandmother" while I tell you a story about Ellen. Ellen's class is learning about how people lived about fifty years ago. Her teacher asked the students to talk to a grandparent or an older neighbor to get more information. Then the students are to write a paper telling what they learned. Ellen talked to her grandmother.

Say:

15. Now listen carefully. Ellen is not sure how to spell the word *television*. She will look it up in the dictionary. Which word will probably be on the same page as television? Is it ...hay ...chicken ...or train? Darken the circle for the word that will probably be on the same page as *television*.

16. Move to the next row. What will Ellen not write about in her paper? Will it be ...How people traveled ...Games people played ...or Where Grandma lives? Darken the circle for what Ellen will not write in her paper.

Say: Now look at the Table of Contents. Listen carefully. Ellen put a Table of Contents at the front of her paper. Read it silently to yourself as I read it aloud. Chapter 1 is called "Food" and begins on page 3. Chapter 2 is called "Games and Toys" and begins on page 9. Chapter 3 is called "Travel" and begins on page 13. Chapter 4 is called "Clothes" and begins on page 20. Now you will answer a question about the Table of Contents. Put your finger under the next row.

Say:

17. What did Ellen write about on page 3? Is it ...long skirts ...milking cows ...or riding horses? Darken the circle for what Ellen wrote about on page 3.

Say: Now go to the top of page 123. Look at what Ellen wrote in the first part of her paper. Read it silently to yourself as I read it aloud.

When Grandma was Young

Grandma lived on a farm when she was little.

The family grew most of their own food.

They grew corn, beans, and potatoes.

Grandma shops at the store on Friday.

They had to raise cows and chickens for meat.

Say:

18. Now place your finger under the next row. Ellen wants to tell how Grandma's family cooked food. Which sentence would she probably write next? Is it ...Grandma cooked food in a big black pan on a wood stove. ... The stove made the kitchen hot in the summer. ...or Grandma helped make bread every day.? Darken the circle next to the sentence Ellen will probably write next about how Grandma's family cooked food.

19. Move to the next row. Which sentence does not belong in Ellen's paper? Is it ... Grandma lived on a farm when she was little. ...They grew corn, beans, and potatoes. ...or Grandma shops at the store on Friday.? Write in the sentence that does not belong in Ellen's paper.

Say: Now look at what Ellen wrote later in her paper. Read it silently to yourself as I read it aloud.

The family could not grow everything they needed.

They had to buy things like flour and sugar.

"<u>Are you ready</u> for some fun?" Great Grandpa
      (1)
would ask.

Then the family knew it was time to go to town.

They would visit <u>mr barton's</u> store.
              (2)

Say:

20. Now place your finger under the next row. Look at the underlined words with the number 2 under them. Did Ellen use correct capitalization to write these words? Darken the circle for the way Ellen should write the underlined words.

21. Move to the last row. Look at the underlined words with the number 1 under them. Did Ellen use correct capitalization to write these words? Darken the circle for the way Ellen should write the underlined words.

Say: Now go to the top of page 124. Look at the picture with the title "Going Fishing." Now listen carefully. Kareem likes to go fishing. Every Saturday he walks to a stream near his house. One Saturday he caught a fish he had never seen before. Kareem went to the library to check out a book about fish. He wanted to find out what kind of fish he had caught.

Say:

22. In which part of the book should Kareem look to find out about the different kinds of fish and to see pictures of fish? Should he look ...in the Table of contents ...on the Title page ...or in the First chapter? Darken the circle for the part of the book where Kareem should look.

Say: Kareem decided to write a story about the fish he caught. Look at the first part of Kareem's story under the title "A Rainbow Fish." Read it silently to yourself as I read it aloud.

A Rainbow Fish

I went fishing.

On Saturday morning.

I caught a fish I have never seen before.

Say:

23. Kareem wanted to describe the fish he caught. Which sentence should he write? Should he write ...Pink and blue stripes the fish had on its body. ... On its body pink and blue stripes the fish had. ...or The fish had pink and blue stripes on its body.? Darken the circle next to the sentence Kareem should write to describe the fish he caught.

24. Move to the last row on the page. Which group of words does not make a complete sentence? Is it ...I went fishing. ...On Saturday morning. ...or I caught a fish I have never seen before.? Darken the circle next to the group of words that does not make a complete sentence.

Say: Now go to the top of page 125. Look at what Kareem wrote later in his story. Read it silently to yourself as I read it aloud.

I did not know what kind of fish it was.

I went to the library to look in a book.

"<u>Where are the books about fish</u>" I asked.
              (1)

The librarian helped me.

I <u>found</u> a picture of the fish.
   (2)

It was called a rainbow trout.

Say:

25. Now place your finger under the next row. Look at the underlined word with the number 2 under it. Did Kareem use the correct word? Should he write ...finding ...finds ...or is it Correct the way it is? Darken the circle for the way Kareem should write the underlined word.

26. Move to the last row. Look at the underlined words with the number 1 under them. Which

punctuation mark should Kareem place at the end of the und erlined words? Write the punctuation mark Kareem should write at the end of the underlined words.

Say: Now go to the top of page 126. In the last part of the test you will find words that are not spelled correctly. Place your finger under the first row. This is Sample F. Look at the sentence. Read the sentence to yourself as I read it aloud.

Flashs of light appeared during the storm.

Darken the circle for the word that is not spelled correctly.

Say: The correct answer is the first word. *Flashs* is correctly spelled f-l-a-s-h-e-s.

Say: Now you will find more words that are not spelled correctly. Do numbers 27 through 34 just as you did Sample F. You have about 10 minutes to complete this part of the test. You may now begin.

Answers: Pages 117–127
Sample A: fish, **1.** sun, **2.** corn, **3.** third picture, **4.** second picture, **Sample B:** made a pitcher of lemonade, **5.** a heron, **6.** "A Mother's Day Surprise", **7.** Possible answer: Janey washed the clothes., **8.** a drum, **Sample C:** Correct the way it is, **Sample D:** On Friday at two o'clock., **Sample E:** The people she will invite, **9.** The muffins were so good that I ate two., **10.** I also drank a glass of orange juice., **11.** think about the food he ate during the day, **12.** to find out if he eats good food, **13.** Correct the way it is, **14.** went, **15.** train, **16.** Where Grandma lives, **17.** milking cows, **18.** Grandma cooked food in a big black pan on a wood stove., **19.** Grandma shops at the store on Friday., **20.** Mr. Barton's, **21.** Correct the way it is, **22.** Table of contents, **23.** The fish had pink and blue stripes on its body., **24.** On Saturday morning., **25.** Correct the way it is, **26.** ?, **Sample F:** Flashs, **27.** leashs, **28.** diging, **29.** bakeing, **30.** walkt, **31.** cryed, **32.** driping, **33.** cherrys, **34.** moveing